BMW
Boxer Twins

Other books by this author:

THE BMW STORY
Racing and production models from
1923 to the present day

Haynes Great Bikes Series
DUCATI 916

DUCATI RACERS
Racing models from 1950 to the
present day

THE DUCATI STORY
Racing and production models from
1945 to the present day

Haynes Great Bikes Series
DUCATI SUPER SPORT

Haynes Great Bikes Series
HONDA GOLD WING

KAWASAKI RACERS
Road-racing motorcycles from 1965 to
the present day

THE KAWASAKI STORY
Racing and production models from
to the present day

MOTO GUZZI STORY
and production models from
the present day

Haynes
Great
Bikes

BMW
Boxer Twins

Ian Falloon

British Library cataloguing-in-publication data:
A catalogue record for this book is available from the British Library.

Published by Haynes Publishing,
Sparkford, Nr Yeovil, Somerset BA22 7JJ, UK

Tel: 01963 442030 Fax: 01963 440001
Int. tel: +44 1963 442030 Fax: +44 1963 440001
E-mail: sales@haynes.co.uk
Web site: www.haynes.co.uk

ISBN 1 85960 963 5

Library of Congress catalog card number 2003 113463

Haynes North America Inc.
861 Lawrence Drive, Newbury Park,
California 91320, USA

Page build by James Robertson, Haynes Publishing
Printed and bound by J. H. Haynes & Co. Ltd., Sparkford.

Contents

Introduction and acknowledgements

Since the release of the R32 in 1923, the boxer twin and the BMW motorcycle have become synonymous. Other manufacturers have emulated, even copied, the design, and BMW has sometimes considered replacing the boxer with an alternative engine layout, but the boxer has endured. Max Friz chose the boxer layout because he felt it was ideally suited for a motorcycle application, and this reason remains relevant today. The two cylinders were out in the airstream for optimum cooling; the engine provided a low centre of gravity, was suited to shaft drive, and could be kept oil-tight. Later designs expanded these features, emphasising reliability and ease of serviceability.

BMW was never afraid to innovate, and the boxer's individuality was highlighted by an adherence to nonconforming features. Pioneered were oil-damped telescopic forks in 1935, and the Telelever in 1993. As other manufacturers were converting to the telescopic front fork, BMW went for the leading link Earles fork. Although it may have followed an alternative path, the boxer always set the standard for all round usability and reliability.

The boxer was also a surprising racing motorcycle, with competition success commencing soon after the release of the R32. Ernst Henne with his world speed records, and the Grand Prix success of Georg 'Schorsch' Meier, provided BMW with unparalleled glory. This continued during the 1950s with the Rennsport, and culminated in multiple sidecar world championships. In 1976, a special R90S won the AMA Superbike Championship, proving the boxer was no longer a sedate touring machine for grey-haired geriatrics. There had been sporting BMWs before, but the R90S was a real Superbike and changed the perception of BMW motorcycles for ever. This

development continued with the equally ground-breaking fully-faired R100RS and dual-purpose R80 G/S, and by 1980 the boxer was on a new path. It failed to die in the wake of the K-series, living again in the R259 of 1993.

Because it possesses a unique character, and provides unparalleled competence over a wide variety of conditions, the BMW boxer has justifiably earned a loyal following. I confess to being one of its devotees. No other motorcycle

6

can compare when it comes to thousands of miles of long-term ownership. From the outset, the BMW boxer was an expensive, high quality machine, often priced beyond the boundaries of mass affordability. This restricted its production numbers and sales for nearly 70 years. Today, with a wider proliferation of models, and more competitive pricing, boxer production has been elevated to unprecedented levels. Whereas it was once limited to a few similar sporting and touring models, now the line-up extends from cruisers to roadsters, luxury tourers, off-road explorers, sportsters, and sport tourers. As the boxer passes its 80th anniversary, the next generation appears imminent, ensuring the continued success of this venerable engine layout.

The preparation of this manuscript has only been possible with the assistance and enthusiasm of many people within the BMW motorcycle community. Fred Jakobs of BMW Mobile Tradition kindly provided information and photographs, and Damien Cook of the BMWMCC, Victoria, Australia, has been unstintingly enthusiastic. Damien shared his knowledge and passion, and I am extremely grateful for his co-operation. Mick Woollett provided many previously unpublished racing photos, and Bruce Armstrong photographed the Daytona-winning R90S Superbike. Other thanks go to Ken Wootton, editor of *Australian Motorcycle News*, Mac McDiarmid, and David Edwards, editor of *Cycle World* magazine, for the use of photographs.

The many enthusiasts who allowed their machines to feature in this book include Julian Barson, Peter Cullen, Neil Earnshaw, Richard Fanning, Lloyd Griffiths, Gerhard Hendricks, Brian Howden, Chris McArdle, Meg Phillips, Martin Preuss, Metzger Rudl, Darryl Suter, Bob Willis, Ken Wright, and Julian Yaxley. Again, thanks go to Mark Hughes and the editorial team at Haynes, and of course my family, who endured many hours of my absence during the preparation of the manuscript.

Ian Falloon
January 2004

Four generations of BMW boxer engines. The A61 of 1993 is on the left, with the A10 from 1992, M268 of 1954, and M33a of 1923. (BMW Mobile Tradition)

1 The birth of the boxer

The first boxer, the R32 of 1923 set BMW on a path that continues today. This example is a 1925 model, not 1923 as described, with a front brake.
(Cycle World)

During the First World War, two companies near Munich's Oberwiesenfeld airport struggled to survive building aircraft and aero engines. One was Gustav Otto's Bayerische Flugzeug-Werke (Bavarian Aircraft Works), and the other was Karl Rapp's Rapp Motor Works. By 1917, Bayerische Flugzeug-Werke was producing 200 aircraft a month, until a fire destroyed the factory and it was reduced to building furniture. Things were little better for the Rapp Motor Works. Following a series of business disasters, it was forced to become a public company, the Bavarian Motor Works, in 1918. Contrary to popular belief, there was no merger between BMW and BFW in 1916, and the two companies continued to coexist until 1922. The merger that year saw BMW move into the BFW premises at Neulerchenfelder Street, later known as Lerchenauer Street. This is still the site of the main BMW works today.

Despite its business difficulties, a talented engineer who had worked with the cantankerous Rapp at Daimler several years earlier gave the struggling Rapp Motor Works a new lease of life. This was Max Friz. During 1917, Friz set about redesigning one of Rapp's problematic six-cylinder aero engines. The resulting IIIa was a triumph, and if it had arrived earlier it could possibly have altered the course of the First World War: certainly in the final days of the conflict Ernst Udet shot down 30 aircraft with his Fokker D VII fighter plane powered by a BMW IIIa. BMW somehow managed to continue the development of a new aero engine, and in June 1919 Zeno Diemer reached an altitude of 9,760m (32,022ft) in a plane powered by the BMW IV engine. However, 11 days later the Treaty of Versailles was signed, forbidding any German company

to be involved in aircraft manufacture.

This provided the impetus for both BMW and neighbouring BFW to seek salvation in other fields of manufacturing endeavour. Coincidentally both companies decided to become involved with motorcycles. During 1920 BMW's foreman Martin Stolle stripped down his 1914 Douglas 500cc flat-twin and Friz set about copying it, with a few modifications. Thus was born the BMW M2 B15 engine. This was then sold to several motorcycle manufacturers as a proprietary motor, including BFW for their Helios early in 1922. Earlier though, in 1920, BFW was involved in the production of the Flink, with a 143cc Hanfland two-stroke engine. However, in the depressed days of 1922 inflation was rampant and the Flink, and later the Helios, sold poorly. When BMW and BFW merged in June that year, BMW inherited the Helios production line and some unsold stock. This encouraged BMW's director Franz-Joseph Popp to engage Friz in motorcycle design, but before he could undertake the design of a completely new motorcycle Friz first redesigned the Helios. He improved the frame, allowing the remaining Helios bikes to be sold, and then set to work on the first BMW motorcycle.

The best method of promoting a new motorcycle, then as now, was to pit it against the competition in racing. In May 1923, Friz successfully rode a prototype R32 in a Munich Automobile Club outing through the Bavarian mountains, and then produced three special overhead-valve versions for the race at Solitude a month later. However, all the engines overheated and the machines failed to finish. By 1924 Friz was back to working on aero engines and the development of racing motorcycles was

entrusted to the 27-year-old Rudolf Schleicher. Not only a competent engineer, Schleicher was an outstanding motorcycle rider, and he rode the prototype overhead-valve R32 to victory in the 1924 ADAC Winter Rally in Garmisch-Partenkirchen, giving BMW their first sporting success. Schleicher would become one of the dominant figures in BMW's racing history through until 1960. For the 1924 race at Solitude he designed a new light alloy overhead-valve cylinder head for the R32, with fully enclosed valve gear. He patented new circumferential

cylinder cooling fins and installed the 500cc engine in an R32 chassis to create the R37. With a claimed 22bhp, the team of three R37s dominated the racing at Solitude, winning all three categories. Rudi Reich set the fastest time, and team-mate Franz Bieber went on to win the German Road Championship that year.

A small number of expensive production R37s was available for 1925. The engine designation was M36a, and compared to the works bikes these produced only 16bhp at 4,000rpm. Despite weighing a considerable

The R32

When it was first launched in Berlin in September 1923, followed by the Paris Car Show a month later, the R32 caused a sensation, and heralded a long line of R-series BMW motorcycles that continues today. Why the designation R32 was chosen is unknown, though 'R' presumably indicated 'Rad', for 'wheel' or 'cycle'. The '32', however, remains a mystery. Although the engine specification was unremarkable, the R32 offered a new level of refinement. Emphasising reliability, with low maintenance, the R32 pioneered a formula that would distinguish all BMW motorcycles. In an era of hand lubrication and messy exposed chains and valve gear, the R32, with shaft final drive and fully encased engine, was a revelation. There was nothing particularly revolutionary about the R32 design; it was just that Friz was the first to combine the features of a horizontal transverse twin with shaft final drive. The Belgian FN had incorporated a cardan shaft final drive as early as 1904, while the British ABC produced a 398cc horizontal transverse twin in 1919.

The engine of the R32 (known as the Type M33a) was based on the Douglas-derived M2 B15, retaining the same 68 x 68mm bore and stroke and one-piece cast iron side-valve cylinder and head layout. With a low 5.0:1 compression and single small 22mm BMW special carburettor, the

power was only 8.5bhp at 3,200rpm. There was a single disc dry clutch, and with its hand-operated three-speed grease-filled gearbox the R32 was considerably more user friendly than other contemporary motorcycles. The only awkward control was the magneto-generator ignition, operated by a complicated set of handlebar controls.

Experience gained from modifying the poor-handling Helios allowed Friz to design a rather heavy, but strong, closed duplex tubular steel frame, with a rigid rear end and short swinging front fork. The front wheel was carried on short trailing arms, with the wheel movement controlled by rods and twin cantilever leaf spring. On early models there was no front brake, and the block rear brake was an old-fashioned type, heel

operated with a dummy belt rim. It was a good thing the 122kg (269lb) R32 was only capable of around 90kph (56mph), but Friz made amends with the second series of 1925 that included a small (150mm) front drum brake. The fuel tank was positioned underneath the upper frame tubes, creating a very distinctive motorcycle. Even though many were sceptical, it was soon apparent that the transverse horizontal twin-cylinder engine layout was ideally suited to a motorcycle. The two cylinders were adequately cooled by the airstream, and the design provided a low centre of gravity that contributed to agile handling. Although the R32 was an expensive, premium quality, luxury product, it was a success and it paved the way for a succession of more sophisticated models.

Although the R32 engine was based on the Douglas-derived M2 B15 design, the R32 incorporated an exposed driveshaft. For the 1920s, it was remarkably oil tight. (Cycle World)

134kg (295lb), the R37 won nearly 100 races in Germany during 1925, including the 500cc class of the German Grand Prix. Racing success gave BMW credibility in Germany, but elsewhere it remained virtually unknown. That all changed when Schleicher took an R37 to England to ride in the Six-Day race. On street tyres, when all the other competitors were fitted with special lugged tyres, Schleicher won a gold medal. This was the first time a German rider had taken a 'gold' in the UK Six-Day event, and the R37 made a significant impression on the specialist motorcycle press.

Also for 1926 the first evolutionary development of the R32 appeared, the R42. The engine (designation M43a) was still a side-valve 500, but with new detachable light alloy cylinder heads, and circumferential cylinder cooling fins. An improved wedge-shaped combustion chamber contributed to a 50 per cent power increase, to 12bhp at 3,400rpm. The frame was similar to that of the R32, but with straight downtubes allowing for a longer wheelbase of 1,410mm (compared to the R32's short 1,380mm). The engine was also located further rearwards to improve handling, while the braking was updated with the introduction of a driveshaft rear brake with narrow brake shoes mounted on the gearbox case. Although it was only produced for two years, the R42 was the most popular BMW motorcycle produced during the 1920s, with over 6,500 sold.

While BMW was earning a reputation for producing solid and reliable side-valve touring machines like the R32 and R42, it continued to develop the 500cc overhead-valve sporting model. In 1927, the R47 replaced the highly

specialised R37, and while this too was a relatively expensive sporting model, it utilised the R42 chassis to keep costs down. The power of the engine (designation M51a) went up slightly, to 18bhp at 4,000rpm, and a significant reduction in price compared to the R37 saw more than 1,700 R47s sold over its two-year lifespan.

Buoyed by strong demand, four new boxer twins were unveiled for 1928, including two 750cc models. There was now delineation between the side-valve and overhead-valve models. The side-valve R52 (M57a) and R62 (M56a) shared a longer (78mm) stroke, while the overhead-valve R57 (M59a) and R63 (M60a) retained the 68mm stroke. Producing 24bhp at 4,000rpm, the R63 was one of the most powerful motorcycles available at the time, and one of the fastest, with a top speed of 120kph (75mph). It also formed the basis of the next generation of racing machines, with both 36bhp and 40bhp versions available to selected clients. At the same time the factory was experimenting with supercharging, and achieved considerable success, with 91 victories through until 1930. Some of the most notable were in the Targa Florio in Sicily. Paul Köppen won this prestigious event in 1927 and 1929, while Ernst Henne won in 1928. The early 500 and 750cc supercharged racers had the centrifugal, and later rotary-vane supercharger, mounted horizontally above the gearbox and driven by an oil-bathed chain from the crankshaft. The power of around 55bhp for the 500 and 75bhp for the 750 was quite extraordinary for 1929, and surely taxed the street-derived tubular-steel chassis to the limit.

During 1927 this overhead valve R47 headed the BMW motorcycle line-up, but it remained a dream for most motorcyclists. (BMW Mobile Tradition)

11

Speed
records

During the 1920s and 1930s, an obsession with world speed records made them even more significant than race track success. Two Englishmen, Oliver Baldwin and Bert Le Vack, were captivating the press during 1928 and into 1929 with their battle to set a new motorcycle world speed record, and Ernst Henne persuaded Friz to allow him to enter into the fray. On 19 September 1929, with a special unfaired short-stroke 750, Henne set a new world record, covering the mile in 134.68mph (216.9kph). However, the record was short lived, as in August 1930 Henne lost it to Joe Wright on an OEC Temple.

With national pride at stake, Henne went after Wright's record, raising it to 137.32mph (221.539kph) one month later. Wright then responded with 150.74mph (242.568kph), and it would be two years before Henne could match that speed. In the meantime, BMW's sales took a downturn: the Depression was beginning to bite, and it was only through product diversification that the company managed to survive.

Fortunately for Henne, Rudolf Schleicher returned to BMW after a brief sojourn at Horch. Schleicher redesigned the record-breaking machine, installing a new multi-plate supercharger to the 750 twin, and in early November 1932 in Tat, Hungary, Henne finally managed to beat Wright's record. He achieved 151.86mph (244.399kph), and would hold the record for the next four years. By 1935, he had raised the record to 169.02mph (256.040kph).

When Eric Fernihough took his Brough Superior to 163.79mph (263.6kph) in 1936, Schleicher responded by preparing a fully streamlined 500 Kompressor for Henne. On

this machine, Henne went 169.01mph (272.006kph), initiating a three-way struggle for the record between Henne, Fernihough, and Piero Taruffi on a Gilera. Henne had the final say to both Taruffi's and Fernihough's new records, when, in November 1937, with wind tunnel tested streamlining for the 90bhp 500, he managed 173.69mph (279.503kph). This record stood for the next 14 years.

During the 1950s, BMW continued its pursuit of world records, with an emphasis on endurance rather than outright speed. Their first post-war record was the nine-hour 500cc, set by Georg and Hans Meier and Walter Zeller at Montlhéry, France, in May 1954. On a specially prepared Rennsport, they managed an average speed of 103.55mph (166.64kph). Later in the year, world sidecar champion Wilhelm Noll set the 10km 500cc sidecar record, achieving 132.17mph (212.7kph).

In October 1955, on the autobahn near Munich, Noll set an absolute world speed

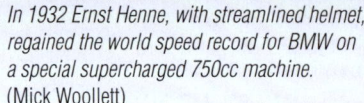

In 1932 Ernst Henne, with streamlined helmet, regained the world speed record for BMW on a special supercharged 750cc machine. (Mick Woollett)

record for sidecars at 174.13mph (280.22kph). His fully-faired, specially prepared fuel injected RS sidecar produced around 80bhp on a mixture of nitromethane and alcohol. Noll also teamed with Fritz Hillebrand and Walter Schneider to claim the 24-hour record. Zeller rounded out a successful few days with a new 500cc 10km solo record at 150.25mph (241.8kph). Although this marked the end of official factory involvement in speed record attempts, several private entries continued to provide BMW with world records. Between 1956 and 1959, Florian Camathias and J.J. Murit set production and sidecar records, with Kasseur, Maucherat, Dagan, and Larivière achieving a 24-hour record for standard machines at 155.3kph (96.6mph) during 1959. Then, in March 1961, London dealer MLG entered a partially streamlined R69S at Montlhéry. Their team of Ellis Boyce, George Catlin, John Holder, and Sid Mizen set a new 24-hour record of 109.36mph (176kph), a record that stood for 16 years.

In November 1937 Henne set a world speed record of nearly 174mph (280kph) with this fully streamlined 500 Kompressor. (BMW Mobile Tradition)

Problems with frame fracture, particularly when fitted with sidecars, prompted the replacement of the R57 and R63 with two new 750cc models in 1929. These were the side-valve R11 and overhead-valve R16, both with a new pressed steel frame. There was no longer a 500cc twin in the line-up, although the R57 continued into 1930. While the engines of the R11 and R16 were carried over from the previous models with few changes, the ugly and heavy riveted frame was all new. There was also a new pressed-steel trailing link front fork, with leaf spring front suspension. Though these new austere machines hardly conveyed sporting prowess, the R11 in particular found favour with the military and helped sustain the company through the difficult period of the early 1930s. 7,500 were produced in five series through until 1934, with the engine designation changing from M56a/1–5. It may have been a workmanlike motorcycle, but the R16 also provided BMW with surprising racing success in the 1933 International Six-Day event in Wales. Showing extraordinary strength and courage, Sepp Stelzer, Henne, Josef Mauermayer, and Ludwig 'Wiggerl' Kraus won the trophy on their cumbersome R16s. With Germany hosting the event the following year, the same team (with R16s) again won the trophy, albeit by a close margin from the Gilera-mounted Italians.

After some difficult years, by 1934 the fortunes of BMW were improving. This coincided with Henne's new world speed records, and led to the release of two new 750cc models for 1935. These were the side-valve R12 and overhead-valve R17, replacing the R11 and R16. The R12 continued the success of the R11, and proved even more popular with the military. Production continued through until 1942, with 36,000 manufactured. Although it shared the utilitarian R12 chassis, the 33bhp R17 (designation M60a/5) was sold as a high-performance sporting machine and was considerably more expensive. Only 434 were produced and it remains one of the scarcest pre-war production models.

The pressed steel frame 750cc side-valve R11 appeared in 1929, lasting through until 1934. Although not beautiful, this austere machine was popular and saw BMW through a difficult period. (BMW Mobile Tradition)

One of the most expensive and exotic motorcycles of the 1930s was the R17. However, combining the obsolete, heavy, pressed steel frame with innovative oil-damped telescopic forks was not a successful recipe. (Ian Falloon)

The 500
Kompressor

With Government encouragement, a new Grand Prix racing motorcycle was developed during 1934 and 1935. This was produced in 500cc (M255/1) and 600cc (M265/1) versions with a supercharger, and M250/1 and M260/1 versions without. However, it was the supercharged 500, the 500 Kompressor, which gave BMW racing glory in the final years before the Second World War.

The Kompressor was one of the most outstanding racing designs of all time, and the engine also formed the basis of the Rennsport solo and sidecar racers that continued to win World Championships until 1974. Compared with earlier BMW racing twins, nothing was shared between the Kompressor and the production versions, with the 66 x 72mm (72.2 x 72 for the 600cc) flat-twin engine featuring lightweight electron magnesium crankcases, and a complicated valve mechanism. Inside each cylinder head were twin camshafts, driven by a set of bevel gears, but as the cylinders were offset the bevel drive lined up with the

Georg 'Schorsch' Meier on his way to victory in the 1939 Senior TT. He was the first foreign rider to win on a foreign machine. (Author's Collection)

exhaust camshaft on the right and the inlet on the left. The second camshaft coupled directly to the driven shafts, but the cams were too close together to actuate the valves directly, so rockers were used. This resulted in a wide included valve angle of 82°. The built-up crankshaft included 140mm one-piece con-rods. Unlike the earlier Kompressor, the Zoller multi-cell vane-type supercharger was now driven from the front of the crankshaft, with a single 27mm Fischer-Amal side-mounted carburettor on the right. This was a far

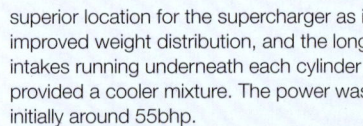

When it appeared in 1935 the 500 Kompressor was fast but was limited by its rigid rear end. (Mick Woollett)

superior location for the supercharger as it improved weight distribution, and the long intakes running underneath each cylinder provided a cooler mixture. The power was initially around 55bhp.

Coupled to the new engine was a four-speed gearbox, with a positive-stop foot change, a first for BMW. Another departure from production models was the tubular steel frame, now electrically arc welded rather than braised as on the earlier tubular frames. Although it retained a rigid rear end, the Kompressor featured innovative telescopic forks with hydraulic damping.

Its inauspicious debut in June 1935, in the hands of Kraus at the Avus circuit near Berlin, provided little indication of the Kompressor's ultimate capability. Ragnar Sunqvist beat it on the Swedish Husqvarna V-twin. Undeterred, Schleicher prepared Kompressors for the 1935 International Six Day Trial, held near Oberstdorf in Bavaria, where the team of Henne, Stelzer, and Kraus triumphed, encouraging further development for 1936.

Acknowledged as the fastest 500, Otto Ley and Karl Gall set about showing that the Kompressor was a match for the superior handling British singles. Finally, in

After the Second World War the Kompressors were brought out of retirement and raced in German events. Development saw upgraded suspension and more power, but they were still essentially pre-war machines. (BMW Mobile Tradition)

August 1936, after a brace of second place finishes, Ley and Gall scored a morale-boosting one–two at the fast Saxtorp circuit to win the Swedish Grand Prix. However, the euphoria was short-lived, as the ISDT team lost the trophy to England after Henne's engine seized twice. The only positive aspect of the ISDT was the success of Alexander von Falkenhausen's new plunger rear suspension.

When the Kompressors lined up at the start of the 1937 season they featured rear suspension, and handled well enough to win four Grands Prix that year. Although BMW was obliged to favour German riders, Englishman Jock West was provided with a Kompressor for the Ulster GP and Isle of Man TT. West rewarded BMW with a victory at Ulster and a sixth in the TT. On this positive note the Germans headed back to England, determined to win the ISDT. This time the 27-year-old Georg 'Schorsch' Meier substituted for Henne, and while he impressed everyone it was the British team which regained the trophy.

Meier's performance in the ISDT earned him a place in the official racing team for 1938, and while he retired at the Isle of Man he won four Grands Prix to take out the European Championship. This wasn't to be Meier's finest hour, however, and although he raced Auto Union cars during 1939 Meier found the time to race at the Isle of Man only a few months before the outbreak of war. This time he won, the first foreigner to win the Senior TT on a foreign machine, and at a spectacular race average of 89.38mph (143.8kph). With West coming second this was a magnificent victory for BMW, albeit marred by the death of their other works rider Karl Gall following a crash during practice.

The works Kompressors were carefully hidden away during the Second World War, but Germany wasn't allowed to compete in international events immediately after the end of the conflict. After 1947, superchargers were banned by the FIM, but this didn't affect the German Championship, so Meier and Kraus resurrected the Kompressor. It proved inspirational, and between 1947 and 1949 the Kompressor

When Germany was re-admitted into the FIM in 1951, the supercharger was removed to create the Type 251 Kompressor. Here Meier leads Zeller at Schotten in July 1951, but Zeller went on to win the German Championship. (Mick Woollett)

(eventually developed to produce around 74bhp) was virtually unbeatable in Germany. The machine was still ostensibly that of 1939, although it had more up-to-date suspension. The leading axle telescopic forks had protective gaiters, as did the rear dampers. Even during 1950 the Kompressor could nearly hold its own against the supercharged NSU twin, but in 1951 Germany was re-admitted to the FIM and the days of the Kompressor were over.

With no replacement immediately available, racing continued with the existing Kompressor, but without the supercharger. Twin carburettors fed the engine (designation M250/2), but the power was reduced to a rather anaemic 43bhp at 8,000rpm. Retaining the telescopic forks and plunger rear end, in the hands of BMW's new star rider Walter Zeller it took everyone by surprise to win the 1951 German Championship. Even in the German Grand Prix at Solitude, Meier, now 41 years old, managed a creditable fourth behind the new 'featherbed' Nortons. But to become competitive in Grand Prix racing BMW needed a new chassis, and responded with the magnificent Rennsport.

Both the R12 and R17 were an amalgam of conservative and radical design. Except for a four-speed transmission, the engines and drivetrain were similar to their predecessors, as was the old-fashioned pressed-steel frame with a rigid rear end. However, the front suspension was by a set of rudimentary oil-damped telescopic forks, the first hydraulic forks to appear on a production motorcycle. While the R12 found a ready market, during 1935 the 500 Kompressor established itself in the racing world and the time became right for a new sporting flagship, with a closer association to the racer. This was the R5, one of BMW's all-time classic designs and the most advanced motorcycle of its day.

A 500cc overhead-valve sporting production model, the R5 was unveiled in early 1936, only a few months after the debut of the 500 Kompressor. Although the arc welded tubular steel frame and telescopic forks were similar to the Kompressor, the engine (designation M254/1) was all new, sharing little with the racer or earlier production models. Central to its design was the one-piece tunnel type aluminium crankcase, a design that would feature on all air-cooled twins through until 1996. Rather than a single camshaft, there were two chain-driven camshafts above the crankshaft, the long timing chain also driving the Bosch generator on top of the crankcase. The included valve angle was reduced to 80°, there were double hairpin valve springs, and the rocker arms pivoted in needle roller bearings.

Like the Kompressor, the four-speed gearbox was foot operated, although the right-hand lever was retained. The power output of 24bhp at 5,800rpm was less than that of the R17, but the R5 was a much more sporting motorcycle, primarily because the weight was reduced to 165kg (364lb). Even with a rigid frame, the handling rivalled the best British singles, and the R5 was certainly one of the outstanding motorcycles of the 1930s. As the R5 was so superior to the R17, a 600cc side-valve R6 joined it in 1937, intended as a replacement for the R12. Strangely, the R6 wasn't simply an enlarged side-valve version of the R5, but featured a completely new engine design (M261/1) with a single gear-driven camshaft. However, while the R6 was an undeniable improvement over the R12, for military sidecar use the older pressed steel frame design was

Not only was the R5 handsome and purposeful, it was one of the best-handling machines of the 1930s. (Ian Falloon)

Boxer
offspring

Many manufacturers around the world were so impressed with the durability of the boxer BMW that they initiated production of similar models under licence. The first of these was the Harley-Davidson XA of 1941–2, a derivative of the R71. 1,000 were produced for the US Army, but the follow-up order for 25,000 fell through due to an aluminium shortage. The Russian Ural of 1943–4 also imitated the R71, and after the end of the war the motorcycle production equipment at Eisenach was transferred to a new factory near Kiev. Again, the result was an R71 derivative, the Dnepr, and during the 1950s the two factories, Ural and Dnepr, developed a wide range of BMW-derived twins, in various capacities and with overhead valves.

Between 1940 and 1944 cylinders for the R12 were manufactured at the Gnome-et-Rhône factory in occupied France, on orders from the German authorities. When the German forces withdrew in 1944 a French company, CMR, assumed control of motorcycle manufacture, and between 1945 and 1946 built a small number of R12-type motorcycles. It also built a few models called the R73, with the R75 ohv engine in the R71 chassis. CEMEC took over the company in 1947, followed by Ratier in 1958, producing the R12-based machine through until 1959, when CSF bought Ratier. Production of a new 600cc ohv model, the C6S, continued until 1962. In nearby Switzerland too, Condor and Universal built similar BMW-derived twins between 1947 and 1968.

The boxer also inspired copies in the Far East, with the Chinese producing an R71-based machine during 1956 with the manufacturing equipment previously used by the Russians. This was called the Chang Jiang, and production continues today, virtually unchanged. The R71-based engine was also used to power a variety of other vehicles and in the 1980s a 750cc ohv version was developed based on the R51/3. Around 12 manufacturers in China produce BMW-based motorcycles, with six manufacturers producing engines.

The Japanese also copied BMW designs, and the 500cc DSK A50 of 1954 was almost an exact duplicate of the R51/3. The Marusho ST 'Lilac' of 1963–7 was initially very similar to the BMW R50, although Marusho continued to develop the design, incorporating telescopic forks and an electric start before BMW.

favoured. As a result the R6 lasted just one year, with only 1,830 produced.

It was inevitable that the production models too would eventually incorporate the plunger rear suspension of the works racers, and four new models with rear suspension were released for 1938. Replacing the R5 and R6 were the similar R51 and R61, while the side-valve 750cc R71 (M271/1) was another attempt to supplant the R12. This time it was more successful, and while the military retained their allegiance to the rigid pressed-steel frame, the R71 continued to sell strongly until production ended in 1941. The R71 was also the final side-valve BMW twin.

The most exciting new motorcycle for 1938 was the top-of-the-range sporting R66. Combining the overhead-valve cylinder heads of the R51 with the superior single gear-driven camshaft set-up of the R6, R61, and R71, the 70 x 78mm 600cc twin (M266/1) produced an impressive 30bhp at 5,300rpm. This was enough to propel the expensive R66 to a top speed of 90mph (145kph), quite an impressive speed for a production motorcycle in 1938. In the final years before the war, BMW also offered racing versions of the R5 and R51 to well-connected privateers. An R5SS appeared during 1937, although this was only a slightly modified R5. Also during 1937 there was a sprung frame R51SS (pre-empting the R51), but

the most effective of these limited edition production racers was the R51RS (Rennsport). Although it retained pushrod-operated overhead valves, this was the closest production model to the works Kompressor. The single camshaft engine (M254/2) was based on the R66, and the power was 36bhp.

With the outbreak of the Second World War military production took priority, and while the R12 continued, development proceeded on a new military motorcycle, the R75 (M275/2). The *Wehrmacht* (German army) had specific design criteria, and the R75 differed from the R12 in that it was conceived with an integral sidecar, with sidecar wheel drive, a locking differential, and cross-country and reverse gears. The 26bhp engine had overhead valves, with two-piece valve covers, while the single camshaft was driven by helical spur gears. The frame was tubular steel, with a central box section and telescopic front forks. By far the most intriguing aspect of the R75 was the differential in the rear wheel housing that drove another driveshaft to the sidecar wheel. As wheel speeds were equalised the R75 had extraordinary ability in difficult terrain. Many other features were also automotive inspired, such as the 16-inch wheels and hydraulic brakes.

Production of the R75 began in Munich in July 1941 but was moved to Eisenach a year later to allow more space for aircraft engine manufacture. Although around 18,000 examples were produced, the R75 was expensive to manufacture and suffered in load capacity compared to the competitive Zündapp KS750 and cheaper four-wheel Volkswagen *Kübelwagen*. The *Wehrmacht* placed its final order for the R75 during 1943, but production somehow continued until bombing in October 1944 heavily damaged the Eisenach factory. After the war, Eisenach was absorbed into East Germany, and motorcycle production recommenced sooner than in Munich.

Bombing also largely destroyed the Munich plant at Milbertshofen, and despite an attempt by Hitler to destroy all military assets early in April 1945, followed by similar American instructions in October, BMW's manager Kurt Donath managed to save the company. By 1948 it was back in business building motorcycles. Initially limited to 250cc, capacity restrictions were lifted during 1949, allowing the production of twin-cylinder motorcycles to recommence. The first post-war motorcycle was the single cylinder R24, heavily based on the pre-war R23, and, with little money available for the development of a twin, the same formula of copying an earlier design was used. Resurrection of the 1938 R51 resulted in the R51/2, which, despite its ancient origins, proved popular during 1950.

There was very little to distinguish the R51/2 from the R51, although the engine (M254/3)

now included the two-piece valve covers of the military R75. Inside the cylinder heads were coil valve springs; the inlet ports and carburettors were angled upwards, but the double camshaft engine layout was the same, inherited from the even earlier R5. Considering the plunger chassis with rudimentary damped telescopic fork was also similar, it said a lot for the innovation of the pre-war design. After only a year there was a new engine, which would power the boxer twin through until 1969.

Although the R51/3 of 1951 looked similar, and provided almost identical performance, to the R51/2, underneath the new smoother and narrower engine cases was an engine (M252/1) more akin to the R6/R66/R71-type. A gear-driven single camshaft above the crank operated the pushrods, and instead of battery ignition there was a Noris magneto on the end of the crankshaft. A special casing above the new gearbox housing contained the paper-element air filter, and while the unremarkable 24bhp at 5,800rpm was the same as the R51/2, the R51/3 proved incredibly popular over its three-year lifespan. Soon a 600cc version, the R67 (M267/1), joined it, with a new bore and stroke of 72 x 73mm. However, this was intended as a utilitarian sidecar mount and only produced 26bhp. Few buyers wanted it, and it became the slightly more powerful R67/2 (M267/2) for 1952. For 1955 and 1956, the R67 continued as the R67/3 (M267/3), still with the plunger rear suspension, but was designed primarily for police duties.

While the R51/2 of 1950 was virtually identical to the pre-war R51, the R51/3 of 1951 featured a completely new engine design. (Ian Falloon)

In the meantime, Germany was officially re-admitted into motorcycle sport. In addition to developing the Rennsport, BMW decided to contest the ISDT for the first time since 1939. Special R51/3s with high-rise exhaust systems were prepared for Meier, Zeller, and Kraus, for the 1951 ISDT held in Varese. This led to the release of a higher performance 600cc sporting motorcycle, the R68, at the end of 1951. First displayed in ISDT trim in anticipation of the Austrian ISDT of 1952, the R68 was one of the finest production BMWs and a true successor to the R66. With a claimed top speed of 100mph, it was a flagship that could meet the best the British manufacturers had to offer. The only downside was the price, and the R68 was unashamedly marketed as an expensive lifestyle accessory.

Based on the touring R67/2, the R68 engine (M268) was more highly tuned. There were higher compression pistons (8:1), a hotter camshaft, and larger 26mm carburettors. A stronger barrel-shaped roller bearing supported the rear of the crankshaft, and there were distinctive new twin rib rocker covers that would last through until 1977 (and were reintroduced in 1992). This development saw the 600cc engine develop 35bhp at a relatively high 7,000rpm.

Ostensibly, the chassis was also the same as that of the R67/2, initially without a sidecar mount. There was a narrow sporting front mudguard, and an optional sprung pillion pad to allow the rider to adopt a more prone riding position. By 1954 the R68 featured light alloy wheel rims and a full width front brake, but remained available only to special order. In Germany the R68 cost 3,950 DM, compared to the 2,750 DM for the R51/3, while in England the price was considered so exorbitant it was unpublished: BMW compared the R68 to the Rolls Royce, so presumably if you had to ask, you couldn't afford it. Most couldn't, and only 1,452 were sold over three years.

The R68 also formed the basis of the 1953 ISDT machines for Meier, Roth, and Zeller in Czechoslovakia, which were hampered by reliability problems. Yet there was substance to BMW's claim that the R68 was the ultimate sporting production motorcycle. In October 1954 Jack Forrest, Len Roberts, and Don Flynn rode an R68 in the first ever 24-hour race for production motorcycles. Held at Mount Druitt, near Sydney, Australia, they managed to avoid a wandering cow that caused several accidents,

ISDT-style high-rise exhaust pipes were an option for the exclusive, high performance R68. (Ian Falloon)

21

The *Rennsport*

During 1952, development of the racing 500 continued, with a new frame providing a lower fuel tank position and allowing swingarm rear suspension. The revised version first appeared on Meier's machine in July at Schotten, and was initially a crudely modified 1951 model. Shortly afterwards, for the race at Riem in Munich, there was a more elegant purpose-built frame. The telescopic forks were retained, and the engine (M253a) was still based on that of the Kompressor, with a single bolt securing the rocker covers. There was experimentation with various combinations of bore and stroke and valve mechanism, one design using a central camshaft underneath the crankshaft, with the valves operated by pushrods and rockers. Other prototypes featured three or four valves in a spherical combustion chamber. The most successful was the M253b, with redesigned cylinder heads and more aerodynamic rocker covers located by two bolts.

In the hands of Meier, Zeller, and Hans Baltisberger, these evolutionary machines were impressive in German events. Baltisberger also gave BMW its first World Championship points with a sixth place in the German Grand Prix, while Meier won the German Championship. The new machine also showed a surprising turn of speed, with Meier setting a lap record of 123.70mph (199kph) at the ultra-fast Grenzlandring.

Development during 1953 resulted in the most successful version the M253/c. Four bolts fixed the rocker covers, and the suspension incorporated leading link Earles front forks. While most examples used twin Fischer-Amal R2A30mm carburettors, Zeller's machine featured fuel injection. Three stages of injector system were tried, the first spraying through the sides of the inlet tracts with the injector nozzle between the throttle slide and inlet port. For the Isle of Man, Zeller's machine featured a new injector system, with the injector located upstream of the throttle, spraying axially into the air trumpets. By the German Grand Prix, Zeller's racer featured long intakes, and injected fuel directly into the cylinder

head. The power for this third stage of injection was claimed to be 61bhp, while the carburetted version produced 58bhp at 9,000rpm. Zeller won the German Grand Prix at the controversial Schotten circuit, but as all the foreign teams declined to race the results were disallowed. Meier and Zeller won several German events but still made no mark on the international scene. All this development, though, led to the release of the limited production Rennsport RS54 for 1954. This proved so expensive to manufacture that only 24 were produced, but they formed the basis of all the factory racers for the rest of the decade, while the engine powered sidecar World Championship machines up until the mid-1970s. Not a bad effort for an engine first designed in 1935.

The 500cc RS54 engine (M253/1) inherited the Kompressor's 66 x 72mm bore and stroke, and the bevel gear-driven double overhead camshaft set-up with short rockers and two straight cut gears in the cylinder head. Also identical was the wide included valve angle. Unlike the factory versions, the production RS54 was in a relatively mild state of tune, and with an 8:1 compression ratio produced only 45bhp at 8,000rpm. A single-plate dry clutch matched to an all-indirect four-speed gearbox. The engine was beautifully constructed, with electron crankcases, and the attention to detail inside the engine was staggering. To minimise cylinder offset, and hence the rocking couple, the crank

With its bevel gear-driven overhead camshafts, the RS engine was one of the most complex of all boxer engines. (Ian Falloon)

featured hollow mainshafts and crankpins, with the middle web of the crank assembly counterbored for the sword-shaped flat section con-rods. Incredibly robust, the engine revved safely beyond 9,500rpm. It may not have been the fastest, but the Rennsport was certainly one of the more reliable racers of the period.

Although first displayed at the end of 1953 with telescopic front forks, the RS54 was fitted with Earles leading link front forks like the 1953 factory racers. There was a new duplex frame, with an oval section backbone, and swingarm rear suspension with the driveshaft enclosed in the right fork arm. At the front was a 200mm twin leading shoe brake, with a 200mm single leading shoe on the rear. While the weight of 130kg (286lb) was moderate, and the performance adequate, the four-speed gearbox and the high-mounted engine handicapped the RS54. Short and top heavy, with the Earles forks increasing the unsprung weight and steering inertia, the RS54 was a very difficult machine to ride. This was accentuated by the torque reaction of the shaft-drive, and as a result most RS54 engines ended in racing sidecars, to which they were more suited.

During 1954, the factory continued to race the Rennsport, with the compression ratio bumped up to 10.2:1 and a five-speed gearbox. Often fitted with a dustbin fairing, Zeller won the German Championship, with victories at Dieburg and Schotten, but there was no joy in international events. Things took a positive turn with von Falkenhausen returning to head the competition department from 1955. Developments saw the driveshaft repositioned alongside the fork leg, not inside it, while remote float bowl Dell'Orto carburettors replaced the fuel injection at slower circuits. The Earles

front forks were also modified to include straight supports (like the production R60 and R69) rather than curved. At the German Grand Prix John Surtees lined up alongside Zeller and Ernst Riedelbauch, Zeller managing second. Zeller won the German Championship again, but could only manage tenth overall in the World Championship. Privateer RS54s were also campaigned with moderate success, and Australian Jack Forrest made an impressive debut at the Imola Gold Cup, finishing fifth

behind the works Gileras and Moto Guzzis. He then took the RS54 back to Australia and at Easter rode it to victory in the Senior TT at Bathurst (with a broken ankle). During 1955, development also commenced on a desmodromic version (M253/d), but this proved unsuccessful.

For 1956, the bore and stroke of the works engines (M253/f) were changed to 70 x 64mm, and former 350cc World Champion Fergus Anderson rode alongside Zeller and newcomer Ernst Hiller. Anderson was killed in an accident at Floreffe in May, but Zeller went to the Isle of Man a month later and claimed fourth place. Running on carburettors, and without streamlining because of the high winds, his race speed was 94.69mph (152.4kph). A steering damper was fitted on the left to improve stability. At the Dutch and Belgian Grands Prix, now with a dustbin fairing, Zeller finished second. A sixth place at Monza, with fuel injection, saw Zeller second overall in the 500cc World Championship behind John Surtees and the MV.

1956 was the high point of post-war BMW solo racing, but unfortunately coincided with a severe downturn in motorcycle sales. With fewer developmental resources now available, results during 1957 were less impressive, although Hiller won several non-championship races. Developments this year included a hydraulic rear brake, and shock absorbers with exposed springs. At the end of 1957 Zeller retired to concentrate on his family steel business, and BMW officially withdrew its support for solo racing. However, it continued to provide machines to selected riders for 1958, and one was the legendary champion Geoff Duke, now without a factory ride following Gilera's retirement from racing.

At the opening World Championship event that year, the Isle of Man, Duke and Dickie Dale had Rennsports with dolphin fairings, and Dale finished tenth. Duke struggled to come to terms with the

Continued overleaf

Ernst Hiller rode alongside Zeller during 1956, and became one of the most successful exponents of the RS. This is Hiller at the 1958 German Grand Prix at the Nürburgring, where he finished fourth. (Mick Woollett)

Dickie Dale at the start of the 1958 Isle of Man Senior TT. He finished tenth, and went on to claim fourth in the 500cc World Championship. (Mick Woollett)

Continued from previous page

handling of the RS, but later rode it to fourth in the Belgian Grand Prix and to victory in the German Championship race at Hockenheim. He then switched back to a more familiar Norton for the World Championship. Dale had more success with the RS, not only winning at Sachsenring but also finishing every World Championship event to take fourth overall. Hiller also continued to impress, finishing fourth in the German Grand Prix and winning the non-championship Austrian Grand Prix.

Although it was obvious that the ageing, and underpowered, BMW was never going to take solo racing glory, Dickie Dale remained faithful to the RS during 1959. He managed only two fourth places, and it was left to promising Japanese rider Fumio Ito to join Hiller on the RS during 1960. In this final development the RS incorporated large dual air scoops for the front brake. With only one points-scoring finish during the year, this was the end for the RS in solo racing, although it was far from dead in sidecars.

Multiple World Champion Geoff Duke at the start of the 1958 Senior TT. Duke struggled with the idiosyncratic RS and their relationship wasn't a happy one. (Mick Woollett)

and won at an average of nearly 60mph (96kph). Forrest, Roberts, and Flynn were favourites to repeat their victory in this event – characterised by incompetent organisation – in 1955, on a new R69, but this time Roberts hit a wandering horse during night practice and was killed, prompting the team's withdrawal.

Two new boxer twins appeared for 1955, the R50 (M252/2) and R69 (M268/2), replacing the R51/3 and R68. Although the engines were largely unchanged, there was a new three-shaft gearbox and diaphragm clutch. Also new was the frame, with swingarm suspension patterned on the RS54 racer. Aimed at improving rider comfort, the front and rear swingarms were controlled by twin automotive-style Boge hydraulic dampers. The driveshaft was now enclosed in the right side of the swingarm, with the universal joint moved to the gearbox end. The R50 and R69 were marketed as reliable, practical, touring motorcycles, with particular suitability for sidecar use. There were interchangeable 18-inch wheels front and rear, and during 1955 sidecar lugs appeared on the R50 frame. The next year saw a touring R60 (M267/4), replacing the R67/3, but it coincided with a serious stagnation in motorcycle sales. This didn't only affect BMW, and during 1957 several German manufacturers (including Adler, DKW, and Horex) disappeared, while BMW's

motorcycle production slumped to less than 5,500. With demand low in Germany, and sales almost non-existent in England due to high import taxes, it was fortunate for BMW that America experienced a surge of interest in sporting motorcycles. In the late 1950s production increased slightly, with 85 per cent of twins going to the United States, but there was virtually no development for five years. With motorcycle line-ups being revamped on a virtually annual basis today, this is difficult to imagine, but it was indicative of the financial problems the company was undergoing. Faced with bankruptcy in 1959, a rally of shareholders helped BMW survive, and during 1960 its motorcycle range was developed and improved, with four new models released for 1961.

Heading the new line-up were two sporting models, the R50S and R69S, alongside new versions of the R50 and R60, the R50/2 and R60/2. The /2s looked outwardly similar to their predecessors, but underneath were a number of developments aimed primarily at improving reliability, notably a stronger crankshaft and camshaft, a new clutch, and closer ratio four-speed gearbox. With a higher compression ratio of 7.5:1, the R60/2 (M267/5) now produced 30bhp (up from 28bhp) at 5,800rpm, while engine specifications for the R50/2 were unchanged.

When Walter Zeller retired from racing at the end of 1957, BMW presented him with this special 500cc supercharged roadster, surely the ultimate road bike of the era. (Mick Woollett)

25

Sidecar racing

While the high-mounted boxer twin with shaft final drive always represented a compromise for solo racing, the reverse was true when it was adapted for a sidecar. And as sidecars developed, the Rennsport engine became even more suitable. It could be mounted extremely low to improve cornering, the engine was smooth with an excellent powerband, the cylinders were adequately cooled, and it was exceptionally reliable. Although there was small scale factory involvement in sidecar racing from 1936 with a 600cc Kompressor in the hands of Kraus and Stelzer, it wasn't until after the war that the boxer achieved real success. Klankermeier and Wolz enjoyed considerable good fortune in Germany with the pre-war machine during 1949, and the next year Kraus and Bernard Huser raced a 900cc version of the wartime R75. Producing around 56bhp, they won the

Wilhelm Noll and Fritz Cron provided BMW with their first sidecar World Championship in 1954. (Mick Woollett)

1,200cc German Championship. With 500cc international regulations in force from 1951, the R51 gained favour for sidecars, while the factory machine of Kraus and Huser was based on the model 251 (plunger frame) factory racer, with a Steib sidecar attached.

It wasn't until 1953 that the BMW twin was a match for the dominant Nortons, when Wilhelm Noll and Fritz Cron finished sixth in the World Championship. For the 1954 season, Noll and Cron had a factory Rennsport (sometimes with fuel injection), with a basic cowling over the front wheel, and more comprehensive streamlining for fast circuits such as Monza. The RS was immediately competitive with the Norton of Eric Oliver and Leslie Nutt, and, with three victories, Noll and Cron gave BMW its first World Championship.

For the 1955 season, BMW fielded three teams, winning every Grand Prix. Although the basic racer was still an RS54 with a sidecar, the Steib sidecar was integrated into the large wide fairing that incorporated two air scoops. The engines were now carburetted, and retained a four-speed gearbox. Willy Faust and Karl Remmert won the World Championship, but Faust retired from racing following the death of Remmert in an accident. Fritz Hillebrand and Manfred

Grünwald replaced Faust and Remmert for 1956, and won the first two Grands Prix on the new, lower sidecar racer. Along with a lower frame, and a reduction in wheel diameter from 18in to 16in, the sidecar was now BMW-built, with a fixed frontal fairing for the bike and platform. This lower, more integrated style would characterise sidecar racers until the kneeling type predominated.

While Noll and Cron won their second World Championship in 1956, Noll's retirement to concentrate on car racing left the championship open for ex-*Luftwaffe* pilot Hillebrand and Grünwald in 1957. Despite Hillebrand's death in an accident in Spain before the season ended, they still won the World Championship. There was only one supported team for the 1958 season, 1957 runners up Walter Schneider and Hans Strauss. While the factory BMW dominated, they were put under considerable pressure from the private Swiss team of Florian Camathias and Hilmar Cecco, who won at Assen. It was a similar scenario during 1959, although the margin was closer as Camathias and Cecco won two Grands Prix.

From 1960, privateers began to match the factory effort, and Helmut Fath and Alfred Wohlgemuth surprised everyone by winning four races on their private entry to take the championship. This year also saw the first kneeler outfit of Fritz Scheidegger, built in an attempt to offset the power differential between his and the factory engines. Although Scheidegger's outfit represented the next generation, he had to bow to the superior power of the factory outfit of Max Deubel and Emil Hörner. Their machine retained a conventional sitting position with the fuel tank above the engine, but they still won the 1961 to 1964 World Championships.

Although Scheidegger's outfit featured disc brakes and small 10in wheels by 1962, it wasn't until the factory's withdrawal at the end of 1964 that he could prove his machine's superiority. With John Robinson he won the 1965 World Championship, repeating this success in 1966. Scheidegger was killed following a brake failure at Mallory Park in March 1967, but Klaus Enders and Ralf Engelhardt took over and gave the BMW twin another World Championship. They lost the title to Helmut Fath and his URS in 1968, but returned the

Fritz Scheidegger was one of the most innovative sidecar racers, pioneering the kneeler outfit. Here, with John Robinson, he is on his way to victory in the 1966 Belgian Grand Prix at Spa. (Mick Woollett)

following year with renewed factory support. With Wolfgang Kalauch, Enders again won the 1970 World Championship, but then decided to retire. The loss of the 1971 title saw Enders return, and with Engelhardt he went on to become the most successful sidecar racer ever, with 27 Grand Prix victories and six world titles. By 1974 his Dieter Busch-prepared RS produced 67bhp at 10,000rpm, with two Dell'Orto carburettors feeding the 70 x 64mm engine. It featured a wide rear car tyre on an Enders-designed wheel, single strut rear suspension, and a very short steering column with a U-link pivoted front fork. There were hydraulically operated drum brakes, with two heavily finned double leading shoes on the front wheel. Weighing 170kg (375lb), it was capable of 245kph (152mph).

Although Enders retired at the end of 1974 in the face of the inevitability of two-stroke dominance, BMW allowed development technician Rudolf Helser to create an updated version with a centre main bearing and four valves per cylinder. Outclassed by the König during 1975, Mike Krauser continued development for 1976. With support from BMW, Krauser had Willi Roth modify the air-cooled boxer engine to incorporate belt-driven twin overhead camshafts and four valves per cylinder. Fuel injected, the engine was restricted to 75bhp because of the FIM-stipulated 110dB(A) noise limit, but it was still capable of 250kph (155mph). Despite the best efforts of Otto Haller and Erich Haselbeck the Krauser machine was uncompetitive, and its best result was sixth at Assen. That marked the end of an era for the RS, that had dominated sidecar racing for so long.

The final BMW racing sidecar engine was this double overhead Krauser version of 1976. Although it sounded magnificent, the four-stroke twin was outclassed. (Mick Woollett)

Replacing the R69 was the sporting R69S (M268/3), with a higher compression ratio (9.5:1), larger inlet ports, a larger volume air filter, and less restrictive mufflers providing 42bhp at 7,000rpm. This was enough to propel the 202kg (445lb) R69S to an impressive 109mph (170kph). The R50S (M252/3) produced 35bhp at 7,650rpm, but at these higher engine speeds proved unreliable and was consequently discontinued after two years.

Although also initially unreliable, the R69S was ultimately one of the most successful post-war twins, and is now hailed as one of the classic BMW motorcycles. During 1962 it received stronger pistons and cylinders to counteract failure. Later in 1963, a rubber-mounted vibration damper was attached to the front of the crankshaft, but this wasn't as successful as anticipated as the unit required frequent maintenance. Generally, though, BMW got the engine right with the /2, and very few developments were required throughout the 1960s. Most small modifications were to the transmission, in an effort to improve the noisy and rather notchy gearshift.

Only a hydraulic steering damper set the chassis of the R69S and R50S apart from the other /2s, and the basic chassis of all models was very similar to the previous R50 and R60. During 1962, frame modifications allowed for the greasing of the rear swingarm bearings without removal. Then in 1964 a grease fitting provided lubrication for the front swingarm bearing. Although they took a long time in coming, these were welcome practical improvements, especially if high mileage was a consideration. The only deficiency in specification was the functionally inferior ball steering head bearings. As with the R50 and R60, there was a choice of large or small fuel tanks, and several seat styles. Traditional black was also not the only colour available, with white, cream, red, teal, blue, and green on offer.

With a price tag of £530 in 1961, the R69S was nearly double the cost of the 650cc BSA A10 Super Rocket in England. As a result it was a luxury sporting machine for the fortunate few, but this didn't deter London dealers MLG from supporting racing and world record attempts. This was initiated back in 1958, when MLG entered an R50 in the Thruxton 500-mile race for production bikes. A fourth place encouraged the team to enter again in 1959, and John Lewis and Peter Darvill won. Later in the same year Darvill, partnered with Bruce Daniels, won the Barcelona 24-hour race. They narrowly failed to win at Montjuich in 1960, but with factory assistance

One of the classic post-war boxer twins, the Earles fork R69S lasted from 1960 through until 1969 with few changes. The large bump on the front engine cover is to provide clearance for the anti-vibration damper. (Ian Falloon)

the MLG R69S won again in 1961. Even in 1964 the BMW twin remained competitive, with Darvill and Norman Price managing a second place. However, during this period the factory was more interested in supporting off-road competition. Its rider was Sebastian Nachtmann, and his factory R50, and later R69S, was used to test new components such as telescopic forks. Nachtmann had some surprising success, including winning a gold medal in the 1960 ISDT.

Although production during the 1960s never managed to replicate the boom years of the early 1950s, the /2 twins sold solidly until 1967. As sales tapered, particularly in the States, specific US models were developed, with a telescopic fork replacing the Earles fork. The latter, while undoubtedly assisting sidecar suitability, contributed to the stayed and old-fashioned image portrayed by BMW motorcycles in the mid to late 1960s; it also imparted strange and idiosyncratic handling characteristics compared to most other motorcycles available at the time. However, since sidecars were now unfashionable BMW reasoned that by simply grafting a telescopic fork onto the existing /2 it would gain a new lease of life. Unfortunately, this didn't eventuate, and the three US market models – the R50US,

R60US, and R69US – failed to generate much enthusiasm. These telescopic fork models were lighter, with improved high-speed handling on bumpy roads, but they looked ungainly. The combination of a high-mounted steering head with the existing low rear loop frame failed to win the hearts of devotees. Although the price of the US versions was barely higher than 15 years earlier, only 3,283 were built between 1967 and 1969. Now they are largely forgotten, and it is the Earles fork versions that are considered the classic BMW twins of this era.

By this stage car production was expanding and becoming increasingly profitable, and the US twins were a belated effort to save the BMW motorcycle from extinction. A remnant of an earlier era, the /2 was also an expensive machine to produce, with lavish attention to detail and finish. The engine, with its built-up crankshaft and gear camshaft drive, didn't lend itself to mass production, and even components such as throttle control and the rear brake linkage were unnecessarily complex. As sales dwindled to around 5,000 in 1968 it became more difficult to justify their existence. The Munich plant was required for automotive expansion, and motorcycle production either had to finish, or move elsewhere.

The standard fuel tank for the 1955–69 boxer twin was a smaller 17-litre (3.7gal) type with integral tool kit compartment, as fitted to this R69S. (Ian Falloon)

2 The boxer revolution

The /5 was the first new BMW motorcycle design for nearly two decades, and the basic design would last for more than 25 years. This is a 1973 R75/5. (Ian Falloon)

During the 1960s Japanese motorcycle manufacturers expanded their horizons, moving into the larger displacement categories and threatening the survival of every other motorcycle manufacturer. Built with up-to-date machinery, the new mass-produced Japanese motorcycles offered class-leading performance and were cheap and reliable. Faced with this Japanese onslaught, and a collapse in European motorcycle sales, BMW almost decided to quit motorcycle production to concentrate on cars.

In spite of this threat, technical director Helmut Werner Bönsch managed to persuade BMW's directors to sanction the development of a new series of motorcycles. The company decided not to compete head-on with the Japanese, but concentrated instead on expanding its traditional boxer-twin trademark.

Although more modern, the new series would remain an expensive quality, luxury touring motorcycle without peer, but would by necessity appeal to a wider clientele than the /2-series.

The design was entrusted to Hans-Günther von der Marwitz, who had joined BMW from Porsche in 1964. Von der Marwitz continued a tradition instigated by Friz and Schleicher, in that he was both an outstanding engineer and an avid motorcyclist. Not a great fan of the Earles fork twins, von der Marwitz favoured the British motorcycle tradition, and held the AJS 7R and Manx Norton in particular in high regard. Consequently when he designed the frame for the new boxer twin it bore more than a passing resemblance to the Manx Norton 'featherbed'.

Once the design was complete, BMW had to find a factory. It already owned a repair and machine workshop in the Berlin suburb of Spandau, and during 1969 this was converted into a motorcycle production facility. While the development and administration remained in Munich, all boxer BMW motorcycles since September 1969 have emanated from Spandau.

The 1970 /5

Central to the new /5 design was an all-new boxer engine (Design M04* or Type 246), which shared little with the previous /2. Typical of BMW's methodical development, this basic engine design was so sound that it survived through until 1996 with only minimal updates. Many features were inherited from successful experience with high performance car engines, including the one-piece forged crankshaft running in plain bearings. Although featured on a prototype twin back in 1932, this was the first production BMW motorcycle engine to include a forged crankshaft with plain bearings. The camshaft was now underneath the crankshaft, with the pushrods below the cylinders, tidying the visual aspect of the cylinders. Also improving the engine aesthetically was the extension of the crankcase to the fuel tank, with aluminium covers for the new electric start, and air filter, on top of the engine. Considerable effort was spent in minimising weight, and instead of the earlier pressed steel sump, the /5 had a cast aluminium sump cover.

Unlike the earlier engine that featured a gear camshaft drive, the camshaft on the /5 was driven by a duplex chain. Drive from the crankshaft was still similar, with a single plate dry clutch mounted to the flywheel, transmitted to a three-shaft four-speed gearbox. The transmission output was through a universal joint, with the driveshaft in the right-side swingarm tube to a set of spiral bevel gears. There were three versions of the /5, 500cc, 600cc, and 750cc, with all variants ostensibly identical, sharing the same stroke but with different bores. The 750cc R75/5 was also the largest official BMW twin since the wartime R75.

While there was no mistaking the heritage of the 1971 /5, underneath the smooth front cover was a chain driven camshaft and alternator. (Ian Falloon)

/5 specifications

	R50/5	R60/5	R75/5
Bore (mm)	67	73.5	82
Stroke (mm)	70.6	70.6	70.6
Capacity (cc)	498	599	745
Compression ratio	8.6:1	9.2:1	9.0:1
Horsepower	32@6,400rpm	40@6,400rpm	50@6,200rpm
DIN/SAE	36@6,600rpm	46@6,600rpm	57@6,400rpm
Left carburettor	Bing 1/26/113	Bing 1/26/111	Bing 64/32/3 (64/32/9 from 1971)
Right carburettor	Bing 1/26/114	Bing 1/26/112	Bing 64/32/4 (64/32/10 from 1971)
Overall width	740mm (29.1in)	740mm (29.1in)	740mm (29.1in)
Seat height	850mm (33.5in)	850mm (33.5in)	850mm (33.5in)
Overall length	2,100mm (82.7in)	2,100mm (82.7in)	2,100mm (82.7in)
Overall length (1973)	2,450mm (84.6in)	2,450mm (84.6in)	2,450mm (84.6in)
Wheelbase	1,385mm (54.53in)	1,385mm (54.53in)	1,385mm (54.53in)
Wheelbase (1973)	1,435mm (56.5in)	1,435mm (56.5in)	1,435mm (56.5in)
Weight including oil but without fuel	185kg (412lb)	190kg (423lb)	190kg (423lb)
Weight including oil and fuel	205kg (452lb)	210kg (463lb)	210kg (463lb)
Top speed	157kph (98mph)	167kph (104mph)	175kph (110mph)

As with all boxer twins since the R5 of 1936, the aluminium /5 engine housing was a one-piece tunnel type, reinforced with internal gussets. The crankshaft was inserted into the crankcase from the front, and while still not featuring a centre bearing (to minimise cylinder offset), strength was achieved by increasing the main bearing journal diameter to 60mm. The three-layer (bronze, tin, and indium) plain bearings were shared with the new six-cylinder 2,500cc BMW car engine, as were the two-piece 135mm steel connecting rods. The big-end journal diameter was increased to 48mm, with a 22mm off-centre gudgeon pin. An automotive-type flywheel bolted on the end of the crankshaft, included a ring gear for the electric start. While still heavy, this flywheel unit was considerably lighter than that of the /2. The /2 always appeared to require winding up, and then would maintain its revs seemingly forever.

Conventional three-ring forged aluminium pistons were fitted to the /5, the flat tops and small valve cutaway promoting good combustion with a moderate compression ratio. To save weight, the cylinders were aluminium rather than cast iron as on the /2. Cast iron sleeves were molecularly bonded to the cylinders through a process called Al-Fin, providing reduced weight and improved heat dissipation. It was a very advanced process for the day, and allowed tighter piston clearances due to the more uniform expansion rates between the piston and cylinder. Underneath the cylinder, the two pushrod tubes also provided an oil return to the crankcase.

Also updated over the /2 was the cylinder head design, with the two overhead valves now located at a shallower, and more up-to-date, 65° included angle. Each version of the /5 came with different sized valves, with the R75/5 having the largest: 42mm intake and 38mm exhaust. The R60/5 valves were 38mm inlet, and 34mm exhaust, with the R50/5 receiving 34 and 32mm valves. The valves were actuated through 22mm hardened followers, pushrods, and rocker arms, with the pushrod having a similar coefficient of expansion to the cylinder to maintain a consistent valve clearance. There were single coil valve springs. As a considerably higher performing model, the R75/5 not only received a longer duration, higher lift camshaft, but a 36mm intake manifold compared to the 26mm manifold of the R60/5 and R50/5.

The camshaft incorporated the drive for the Eaton oil pump at the rear, with the ignition advance unit and tachometer drive at the front. To the dismay of purists, instead of the earlier helical timing gears the camshaft drive was also inspired by BMW car engines. This was now by a duplex 3/8 x 7/32in chain, and incorporated an automatic leaf spring tensioner developed for racing sedans. The chain camshaft drive was an undoubted economic necessity, and was less noisy, but it wasn't as reliable as the earlier gear set-up.

Considerably upgraded over the /2 was the lubrication system. As the plain bearings required copious amounts of filtered high pressure oil, there was an Eaton hypo trochoidal pump, capable of delivering 370 gallons (1,400 litres) per hour at 6,000rpm. The oil pump sucked oil from the oil pan, and pumped it through the main lubricating passages into the automotive disposable full flow oil filter. The timing chain was splash lubricated from the sump, and a venting dome on top of the crankcase separated the oil mist from crankcase pressure through a check ball valve feeding back into the intake. Apart from some minor development to the oil supply passages during 1979, this lubrication system remained unchanged throughout the life of the engine, and undoubtedly contributed to its extraordinary reliability.

Also new was the rather convoluted air intake system, with the air filter inside the rear engine cover above the gearbox, rather than in a separate housing as on the /2. Underneath the fuel tank was a rear facing air intake grille. Although it provided no ram air effect, the air filter volume was 60 per cent greater than that of the R69S. A small amount of air went to cool the electrical components on the front of the engine before the filtered air entered a common chamber under the large disposable dry paper air filter. Air then proceeded to two individual carburettor ducts, successfully quieting the intake noise and providing excellent air filtration, if not contributing to horsepower.

While the R50/5 and R60/5 retained the earlier type of Bing 26mm concentric carburettor, the R75/5 included a new type of Bing 32mm vacuum carburettor. The concentric carburettor didn't include a choke, only an enriching float plunger, while an accelerator pump supplied additional fuel. On the vacuum carburettor the choke lever was positioned on the left of the air filter housing.

One of the most significant developments over the /2 was the electrical system. The six-volt magneto system of the /2, virtually unchanged since the R51/3, was decidedly antiquated by 1969. For the /5 there was a 12-volt electrical system, with an automotive-type three-phase alternator positioned on the end of the crankshaft. Designed by BMW and built by Bosch, this alternator provided a modest 180W, with a maximum current of 13 Amps. A small 15Ah battery powered the electrical and ignition system, with a single contact breaker opened by a cam incorporated on the end of the camshaft. As the automotive-style engine layout lent itself

The R75/5 was the first official 750cc BMW since the wartime R75. 1970 and 1971 examples like this had dual passenger grab handles. (BMW Mobile Tradition)

to electric starting, a Bosch 0.5bhp electric start motor was positioned above the crankcase, hidden underneath a removable alloy cover. The electric start was standard on the R75/5 and R60/5, and optional on the R50/5, while the traditional sideways kick-start was incorporated at the back of the gearbox, connecting to the input shaft. Despite the small battery, starting was reliable, although the penalty was weight, with the electric start assembly weighing around 50lb (23kg). The electric start considerably widened the appeal of the boxer twin, with those previously daunted by the idiosyncratic kick-start now considering a BMW for the first time.

A 180mm single disc dry clutch connected the crankshaft and the transmission input shaft, with a diaphragm spring compressing a pressure plate and bonded clutch plate. The more powerful R75/5 had a thicker and stronger clutch spring. Also new for the /5 was the all-indirect three-shaft four-speed gearbox that mounted directly to the engine housing.

All /5s were fitted with leading axle telescopic forks, and the front brake sidecover on the left was chrome-plated.
(Ian Falloon)

Although the gearbox shifted more smoothly than earlier BMW twins, it still came under criticism, and there were continual modifications to the shifting mechanism over the next few years. There was an enclosed driveshaft running in an oil bath in the right side of the swingarm, with a universal joint at the gearbox end, bolted to a drive flange mounted to the taper of the transmission output shaft, with a hypoid gear coupling at the input end. On the rear of the driveshaft was an internally splined coupling to facilitate ease of wheel removal, but this was particularly prone to wear. The rear drive was through a set of familiar and well-proven helical tooth spiral bevel gears, with each /5 version receiving a different set of final drive ratio.

It wasn't only the engine of the /5 that represented a significant departure from previous boxer twins. Von der Marwitz was intent on creating a motorcycle that handled in the manner of a Manx Norton, so the chassis (also Type 246) was also new. And for the first time the frame was designed exclusively for solo use, and sidecars weren't considered. As it didn't need to support a sidecar the frame was much lighter than before, and comprised a 45 x 3mm diameter dual walled backbone attached to double loops that varied from 28 x 1.5mm diameter to 32 x 3mm. 4mm gussets braced the 46 x 4.5mm diameter steering head, permitting controlled longitudinal elasticity without affecting torsional rigidity. The variable section conical tubing included changes in taper and ovality in accordance with the anticipated stress, and was argon welded. It weighed only 13kg (28.6lb), significantly less than the 17.5kg (38.6lb) of the /2 frame. The tunnel for the fuel tank was very shallow, and a light triangular steel rear subframe bolted to the main frame with four 8mm bolts. As the rear shock absorbers attached to this bolted-on subframe, this was another area of weakness.

Because of the inherent flexibility and bolted subframe, the strength of the structure was questioned, but the design remained essentially unchanged until 1996. Von der Marwitz was convinced too much frame stiffness was detrimental for a street motorcycle, and the frame earned a reputation for flex that soon provided the /5 with a new nickname, *Gummi Kas* ('Rubber Cow'). Stability deficiencies could be overcome with tyres with stiffer sidewalls, but the chassis still felt a lot looser than that of other European motorcycles. The short swingarm, pivoting in the frame on strong adjustable tapered roller bearings, also impaired stability, and this was lengthened during 1973.

From the R50US, R60US, and R69US of 1967–9 came the Sachs manufactured (to BMW specification) telescopic fork. While featuring a forged aluminium lower fork yoke, another cause of handling instability was the flimsy pressed-steel upper fork yoke. The 36mm front fork, though, was relatively sophisticated, with the leading axle design allowing for longer springs and dampers. The trail of 93mm (3.62in) was also obtained with a triple clamp providing less offset, technically desirable as it minimised steering head inertia. With conically tapered damper tubes, the fork was functionally superior compared to most available in 1970, and the spring travel of 208mm (8.2in) was exceptional for a street motorcycle. While the long travel and soft springs aided comfort, it inhibited ultimate sporting ability, as it provided considerable dive and weight transfer under hard braking. The fork design, however, was sufficiently advanced that it was retained until the introduction of the K-series type on the R80 and R65 in 1985. Another improvement over the /2 was the incorporation of tapered roller bearings in the steering head. There was a friction steering damper, with a knob adjuster on top of the upper fork yoke, but a more effective hydraulic steering damper was available as an option. Twin 316mm (12.3in) rear Boge shock absorbers were fitted, also providing generous travel (125mm/4.92in). There was an alloy cover over the top of the spring, and spring preload adjustment was by a lever incorporated at the bottom of the shock absorber.

As a premium motorcycle, many high quality components distinguished the /5. The 1.85 x 19in front and 1.85 x 18in rear wheel rims were aluminium instead of the more usual chrome-plated steel, with a special stamp to lock the tyre to the rim. Even the wheel bearings were a more durable special sealed tapered roller type. As a conservative company, BMW resisted the trend towards disc brakes and fitted the /5 with new, narrower and more rigid, drum brakes. With bonded brake linings developed for the last Porsche cars with drum brakes, the alloy housings incorporated deep stiffening and

Many features of the /5 were modern, but the single face instrument layout in the headlight, and the universal plunger ignition key, were distinctly old fashioned. (Ian Falloon)

cooling ridges. At the front was a 200 x 30mm Duplex (double leading shoe), with a 200 x 30mm Simplex (single leading shoe) on the rear. The front brake looked less cluttered than many double leading shoe designs as there was a single adjustable rod between the two front brake pivot arms, with both arms pulling in the same direction. The single brake cable attached directly to the arms, moving them together when the front brake lever was pulled. The system worked well enough, and when properly adjusted the front brake was perfectly adequate if not exactly overwhelming. Rear brake actuation was by a rod and both brakes included garish chrome-plated covers on the left side. Other high quality fittings included Magura forged aluminium levers with finger indentations and Teflon bushings, the /2-type cam, and chain throttle.

With its large 22-litre (4.8-gallon) fuel tank straddling the frame the /5 imparted a completely different impression to its predecessor, but continued a tradition of exceptional quality. The paint was impeccable, and the hand pinstripes fastidiously accurate. There were also rubber knee pads incorporated on each side, and the /5 was the last BMW motorcycle with the traditional fired cloisonné enamel BMW emblems that screwed into the tank. Although also available in other colours, most pre-1969 BMW twins were black with white pinstripes, but the /5 broke this tradition with many now in silver (with blue pinstripes) or white (with black pinstripes). Matching the tank were lightweight fibreglass mudguards.

35

Above: Hans-Otto Butenuth on his way to fourth place in the 1971 Isle of Man Production TT. (Mick Woollett)

Below: Helmut Dähne rode this special-framed R75/5 to 13th place in the 1972 Imola 200-mile race. The carburettors are large Dell'Orto SS. (Mick Woollett)

Racing R75/5s: *Dähne and Butenuth*

While the MLG R69S provided some success for BMW in endurance racing in the early 1960s, the R69S was basically unsuited to road racing. Although reliable, it was solid and heavy, and not blessed with exceptional power. The Earles forks also provided distinctive handling that didn't suit everyone. But this all changed with the release of the /5. Not only did the /5 handle better than the /2, the engine design was considerably stronger. Von der Marwitz gave BMW a motorcycle that had real sporting potential, and could acquit itself in production and production-based racing.

The R75/5's chief exponents in Europe were Helmut Dähne and Hans-Otto

Dähne with the F750 R75/5 at the Imola 200 in 1973. (Mick Woollett)

Butenuth. After joining BMW in 1959 as an apprentice mechanic, Dähne rose to become a development engineer and test rider. He began racing seriously in 1968, and during 1970, still as an amateur, Dähne won the German B-grade Championship. He applied to ride his R75/5 in the 1971 Isle of Man Production TT but was rejected by the British ACU because it didn't consider him experienced enough. Other R75/5 entries were accepted, including Dähne's friend and fellow factory-supported rider Hans-Otto Butenuth. Butenuth won the 1971 German Championship on a special factory-prepared RS, and finished fourth in the production TT on an R75/5. The private machines of Tom Dickie and Tony Anderson managed seventh and ninth. It was a promising result in a field dominated by Triumphs and Nortons.

With the advent of Formula 750 in 1972, Butenuth and Dähne entered the inaugural Imola 750 in April on special R75/5s, developed with unofficial factory assistance. Although outpaced by the horde of factory teams, Dähne and Butenuth put up a good showing. Dähne's machine had a narrower GP-style frame, shortened forks, and an engine fed by Dell'Orto carburettors. His 13th overall result earned him his first ride in the TT. Armed with his F750 machine, as well as the production R75/5, Dähne managed fourth in the 1972 Production TT, and 11th in the F750 race. Dähne continued to develop his R75/5 during 1973, retaining the short wheelbase frame from 1970. This year he came 14th at the Imola 200, while repeating his fourth place in the Production TT and moving up to ninth in the F750 race. 1973 was the final year for a 750cc limit in the production TT, but BMW already had the R90S waiting for 1974. And in preparation for the R90S, a special version came third in the 1973 Bol d'Or.

Still riding a short wheelbase R75/5, Dähne managed fourth place in the 1973 Production TT. (Mick Woollett)

Although the /5 was a significant step forward for BMW, it retained a number of unusual and eccentric features. The Hella handlebar switches were not very ergonomic, and the unfused headlight flasher presented a fire risk. Most surprising was the retention of the obsolete universal plunger ignition switch, a feature since 1936. Every BMW motorcycle until 1974 would operate with the one plunger key. Another old-fashioned characteristic was the instrument cluster incorporated in the headlight shell. Despite these rather quaint elements, the /5 impressed even the most sceptical when it was shown to the world's press at Hockenheim at the end of August 1969. Production of the R60/5 commenced in September that year, followed by the R75/5 in October and the R50/5 in November. The /5 was so successful that motorcycle production for 1970 nearly trebled, to 12,287, after slumping to only 4,701 in 1969.

The 1971 and 1972 /5

As von der Marwitz's development of the /5 was exhaustive, there were only minimal updates to the /5 series for 1971. The sharp-eyed could pick the turn signal light added to the left of the ignition switch in the headlight, while to improve the R75/5's idle there were new carburettors. To sharpen acceleration, the R75/5 also received a lower final drive ratio.

Many more changes appeared for the 1972 model year. This was the year of the 'toaster' tank and chrome-plated battery covers, but there were also a number of other developments. The engine received a stronger crankcase and an upgraded crankshaft, with new bearing shells. The styling makeover centred on a new 17-litre (3.7-gallon) fuel tank, with garish chrome-plated side panels and matching chrome-plated battery covers. Intended primarily for the American market, this was soon nicknamed the 'toaster' because of its similarity in looks to the kitchen appliance. Along with the smaller fuel tank there was a new seat, with a single handrail instead of the double handrails of the 1970 and 1971 models. While the frame was unchanged, the side stand was now spring-loaded, and annoyingly self-retracting. One of the more significant improvements for 1972, though, was to the front fork. To reduce fork stiction there was now a three-piece floating damper nozzle instead of the earlier fixed bushing. The rear

During 1973 the /5 received a longer swingarm, providing noticeably increased space between the battery and rear mudguard. (BMW Mobile Tradition)

39

There is no denying the elegance of the R75/5, some of which was lost with the later /6 and /7. Today the /5 is considered one of the more collectable modern BMW motorcycles.
(Ian Falloon)

wheel rim was also increased to a wider WM3 2.15B x 18in.

The 1973 /5

The radical styling of the 'toaster' wasn't well received, and it was discontinued for 1973. The larger fuel tank was now standard, but the smaller tank (without chrome panels) and the battery panels (also painted) remained an option. There were a few small engine updates (to the oil pump and centrifugal advance unit), but the most significant development was a longer swingarm, fitted from January 1973. Not only did this lengthen the wheelbase, improving stability, but it also allowed for a larger battery and a longer seat. But it was obvious that this longer swingarm was a precursor to the /6-series already in the developmental stages. Two of these longer wheelbase R75/5s were selected at random from the production line by the West German Motorcycling Federation and shipped in sealed cases to the Isle of Man in May, in an attempt to win the coveted Maudes Trophy. Only awarded to manufacturers for extremely commendable performance, and run under strict ACU control, 14 riders rode the two R75/5s continuously for a week. Despite heavy rain, and two crashes, the two machines covered 16,658 miles and won the Trophy.

The /5 saved the BMW motorcycle from extinction, but was already outdated in a number of areas. By 1973 many larger displacement motorcycles had a front disc brake and a five-speed gearbox. Most customers expected a console with separate speedometer and tachometer, and they certainly demanded an ignition switch specific for the motorcycle. On 28 July 1973, only three days after the 500,000th BMW motorcycle (an R75/5) had come off the Spandau production line, the last /5 was built. The demise of the R50/5 also saw the end of the venerable 500cc boxer twin, initiated with the R32 back in 1923. However, by 1973 the demand for a 32bhp, 205kg motorcycle was diminishing, and R50/5 production only numbered 7,865 (compared to 38,370 R75/5s).

Although the /5 was supplanted by the improved /6, as with the /2 it too represented the end of an era. With the /6 came a quest for more economic construction, with a plethora of plastic components replacing those previously made from metal or enamel. Despite the relatively large number manufactured, each /5 was still painstakingly crafted, continuing the tradition of the /2. But as motorcycle production continued to grow it was inevitable that the quality couldn't emulate that of the earlier machines. Apart from a few early /6s, the /5 was the last BMW motorcycle with enamel tank badges, and featuring exceptional paint, chrome, and fittings on a mass-produced motorcycle. Later boxers offered improved performance, but as production levels increased something intangible was lost.

Although it combined traditional and modern features, by 1973 the R75/5 was becoming outdated. (Ian Falloon)

The
Butler &
Smith
R75/5
racers

While Dähne and Butenuth were campaigning the R75/5 in Europe, US BMW distributors Butler & Smith watched their progress with interest. /5 sales stagnated in the US during 1971, and Butler & Smith president Dr Peter Adams reckoned racing could halt the slide. The AMA Championship was also to be run under F750 regulations for 1972, and it seemed a good opportunity to produce an R75/5-based racer. Development was entrusted to West Coast service manager Helmut Kern, assisted by Matt Capri and Miles Rossteucher. Kern managed to obtain special parts through his contacts within the factory, while BMW's American representative Volker Beer supplied a racing frame similar to Dähne's. The resulting racer was commendably narrow, but didn't handle as well as expected as the frame wasn't sufficiently strong around the steering head. Kurt Liebmann rode this R75/5 racer throughout 1972, including the 100-mile Junior race at Daytona. He failed to finish, but Kern reasoned that the R75/5 was more suited to the emerging class of production racing.

Kern began with Adams's 1971 model R75/5, and hired Reg Pridmore to ride in the 1972 West Coast Production series. Initially there were few developments. A 19in wheel was fitted on the rear, and the cylinders shaved to increase the compression ratio. During 1972 and 1973 the engine received shorter con-rods, 10.8:1 Venolia pistons, rockers pivoting on needle rollers, Jerry Branch ported cylinder heads with 42mm inlet valves, hollow tappets, and aluminium pushrods. The flywheel was heavily drilled to reduce weight, and tungsten plugs were inserted in the crankshaft. Just about all these racing developments eventually found their way onto the production models, once again demonstrating that racing improves

the breed. While the chassis was stock, Kern spent considerable time and effort reworking the front suspension. The result was possibly the most effective production racing motorcycle in the United States during 1972 and 1973. Pridmore managed 15 wins and six second places out of 23 starts, but as the series was confined to the West Coast it had limited exposure. Butler & Smith also returned to Daytona in

1973 with F750 machines for Liebmann and Pridmore, but they were completely outclassed.

For the 1974 Daytona 200-mile race, Butler & Smith came with two revised machines featuring frames built by Englishman Rob North, who emigrated to Southern California during 1973. At Pridmore's instigation Kern approached North to provide a frame similar to those of

Left: Kurt Liebmann on the Rob North-framed Butler & Smith racer at Daytona, 1974. (Mick Woollett)

Right: Liebmann rode the North-framed F750 bike at Daytona in 1975, but it was completely outclassed. (Mick Woollett)

his highly successful Triumph and BSA 750cc triples. North subsequently built two frames, and they were closely patterned on the Triumph version, except for a higher engine location and a longer swingarm. The resulting wheelbase was quite long, at 1,470mm (57.9in), but the double-cradle chrome-molybdenum steel frame was strong and immediately tamed the handling of the R75/5. The driveshaft also ran in the right side of the swingarm, but with an exposed U-joint to save weight.

The 750cc engine was based on Pridmore's successful R75/5 production racer, with input from many of California's leading hot rod exponents, and was further developed throughout 1974 and 1975. Jerry Branch reworked the cylinder heads with 44mm intake valves, and straight intake ports as the carburettors no longer needed to clear the rider's shins, while Sig Erson developed the camshaft. To minimise power loss, the camshaft drive was initially by a single-row chain. However, as revs increased and heavier valve springs were required, the chain sprockets failed and the duplex chain was reinstalled. Carburation was by Mikuni, initially 38mm but later reduced to 36mm. The 83mm 12:1 pistons were Venolia, and their altered gudgeon pin location allowed each cylinder to be 14mm shorter, improving ground clearance. Ignition was electronic Krober, with twin spark plugs per cylinder, two triggers, and four coils. The crankshaft rod journals incorporated a second oil supply hole, and weight saving extended to lighter counterweights (by 80g) and removal of the generator. The con-rods were titanium, and to improve throttle response the standard flywheel was drilled to weigh only 1.6kg (from 3.6kg). The larger sump carried another 1.1 litres of oil, and a Triumph oil cooler controlled the temperature at 9,500rpm. By 1975 the 750cc engine produced 92bhp. During 1973 the AMA

sanctioned five-speed gearboxes, but as the R75/5 only featured a four-speed gearbox a five-speed Kaiser-converted unit was used. By 1975 the gearbox was a BMW unit, but with a drum shifting mechanism instead of cam-plates. There was a choice of eight final drive ratios, ranging from Daytona's 1:2.75 to a 1:4.25 for the twisty Sears Point circuit.

Over its two-and-a-half-year developmental period, East Coast Racing Director Udo Gietl spent a lot of effort on the suspension. The racing Ceriani forks, similar to those of the racing MV Agustas, had Betor triple clamps, and the twin Girling shock absorbers featured heavier damping with light springing. This was found to suit the peculiar characteristics of shaft drive, and the resulting steering and handling were impeccable. During 1975 Gietl also experimented with monoshock rear suspension. The wheels were Morris magnesium, with double 230mm drilled cast-iron disc brakes with dual-piston Lockheed calipers on the front, and a single disc on the rear. At 140kg (309lb) the B&S racer was lighter than the Yamaha and Suzuki two-strokes, and capable of 265kph (165mph).

The North-framed machines were hopelessly outpowered at Daytona in 1974,

with only Pridmore qualifying. It was rumoured Pridmore's machine displaced 1,000cc, but his retirement with a cracked valve while in 12th position eliminated the embarrassment of a post-race teardown. The B&S machines were effective enough in regional races on bumpy tracks, and Pridmore put the bike on the front row at Laguna Seca. He also proved its potency in out-accelerating the Yamaha 700s at Road Atlanta. Even when four-strokes appeared dead in AMA racing, Butler & Smith entered Liebmann on an F750 racer in the 1975 Daytona 200.

Now at the peak of their development, by 1975 the F750s were producing around 100bhp at the crank and running to 10,500rpm, and were probably the fastest pushrod twins ever created. Although top ten finishers in AMA Nationals, and faster than the once-dominant Harley V-twins, they were an anachronism. Both the Butler & Smith racers have survived, one in Orange, California, in the collection of Evan Bell, while the other is on display in the Barber Vintage Motorsports Museum in Birmingham, Alabama. They remain testimony to the magnificent era when BMW in America was committed to racing, against all odds, and when racing development trickled onto production bikes.

③ Superbike

One of the few modern production BMW motorcycles to have become a classic is the R90S. (Ian Falloon)

The /5's buoyant sales having ensured that the future of BMW motorcycles was secure, the next stage in development was to build on its racing success. Helmut Dähne, Hans Otto Butenuth, and Reg Pridmore had shown the R75/5 to be a formidable production racer, and this led to the first BMW Superbike, the R90S. The impetus for the R90S came from Bob Lutz, BMW's American-born sales director, also responsible for the unloved 1972 'toaster' tank /5. Lutz planned to radically change the image of BMW motorcycles, and while the 'toaster' was a flop, the R90S was a huge success. It was also more than just a high performing R90/6; it was an aesthetic triumph, a stylist having been employed in the motorcycle division for the first time. This was Hans A. Muth, who came from Ford and initially shared his time with the

Racing
the R90S

Although Helmut Dähne left BMW to work for Metzeler in 1974, he maintained his relationship with BMW, and with the assistance of Helmut Bucher continued to develop his older R75/5 racer. With the production TT capacity limit now 1,000cc, Dähne installed a new 900cc engine with five-speed gearbox in the older short wheelbase chassis, along with a dual disc front end. The boxers were now contenders for victory, and in the 1974 Isle of Man production TT Dähne came third, behind Mick Grant's Triumph and Hans-Otto Butenuth. Butenuth's R90S was a special 1,000cc version developed by Paul Blum.

Dave Potter also rode a Gus Kuhn F750 version of the R90S at the Imola 200 in 1974, but four-strokes were totally outclassed by this stage.

The 1975 Production TT was a ten-lap handicap race with two riders, and Dähne teamed with Werner Dieringer. After two laps, Dähne was in the lead when he knocked a hole in the right-side cylinder head cover, losing all the engine oil. He managed to finish ninth in the Open Classic TT on the same bike later in the week, the first four-stroke home, and his lap of 101.89mph (163.94kph) was the first 100mph lap for a BMW at the Isle of Man.

Dähne returned to the Isle of Man in 1976 with the engine trimmed 22mm (0.9in) on each side to improve ground clearance. This was achieved through special 10.5:1 Mahle pistons with raised gudgeon pins, and shorter con-rods. With a sporting camshaft,

and ported cylinder heads, the production R90S produced 80bhp at 7,000rpm. The crankshaft and flywheel were lightened, and there were lighter, thinner, alloy pushrods, enabling the engine to rev safely to 8,000rpm. The weight of the Daytona Orange R90S was reduced to 185kg (408lb), and, teamed with Butenuth, Dähne led the 1976 Production TT from start to finish, averaging 98.82mph (159.0kph). However, under the handicap system they were credited with fifth, the first time the fastest finishers didn't win a TT. Dähne's fastest lap of 102.52mph (164.95kph) remains the best ever lap of the Isle of Man by a pushrod boxer twin, and he and Butenuth were the moral victors.

Dave Potter astride the Gus Kuhn F750 R90S at the 1974 Imola 200. The chassis was surprisingly standard, and the machine uncompetitive. (Mick Woollett)

BMW automotive division. The R90S was his first motorcycle effort for BMW.

Heading the new /6 line-up, the R90S shattered for ever the perception of BMW motorcycles as staid and stodgy touring machines. It represented a new direction, combining innovative styling, class-leading performance, and supreme refinement. And for the only time in the history of BMW production motorcycles, the R90S's performance was comparable to that of any motorcycle produced in Japan, Italy, or England. Consequently the R90S commands a special place in the annals of BMW motorcycles. Subsequent air-cooled boxers provided superior handling and braking, some were faster, but the R90S was the pioneer, and it remains the classic post-1970 boxer. Released alongside the R90S in October 1973 was the /6-series, a continuation of the /5 concept but with the more modern updates of a five-speed gearbox, disc front brake (on the larger models), dual instrument console, and a powerful H4 halogen headlight.

In 1974 the R90S set the standard for sport touring motorcycles, and only the R90S had a cockpit fairing that included full instrumentation. 1974 models retained the kick-start and /5 handlebar switches.
(Ian Falloon)

The 1974 R90S, R90/6, R75/6, and R60/6

Although the basic engine housing was carried over from the /5, the crankcase was strengthened around the front aperture. The model type was 247, with all /6s retaining the existing 70.6mm stroke. On the two 900cc versions, 90mm pistons increased the displacement to 898cc. In 1974 these were amongst the largest pistons fitted to a production motorcycle, and the bore/stroke ratio of 1:1.27 provided by the oversquare engine dimensions was quite radical. Visually setting the /6 apart from the /5 were a new outer alternator and ignition cover, and inside the engine was a new crankshaft. On the R75/6, R90/6, and R90S, this included the smaller crank counterweights and tungsten plugs, originally tested on the Butler & Smith racers. To improve heat dissipation, the aluminium cylinders of the R90S were painted black. The two 900cc versions received larger (40mm) exhaust valves, while retaining the 42mm inlet valves, but the engine specifications for the R75/6 and R60/6 were identical to their /5 predecessors. Instead of the bronze bushes, all /6s included needle roller bearings for the rockers, also as tested on the B&S R75/5 racers.

The additional power of the R90S over the bread-and-butter R90/6 came from higher compression pistons and larger carburettors. Unlike the time-honoured Bing, the carburettors were Dell'Orto, long favoured for racing RS engines. Although Ender's sidecar racer used remote float bowl concentric Dell'Ortos, the R90S featured the more recent concentric PHM type, with accelerator pumps. The 38mm throat diameter was also much larger than that of the carburettors for any previous BMW motorcycle. Considering the mufflers were still exceptionally quiet, the power output of the R90S was extremely impressive.

Upgraded over the /5 was the electrical system. Both the R90S and /6 received a higher output three-phase Bosch alternator, with that for the R90S having a smaller outside diameter. This was to provide clearance between the stator and alternator for crankshaft whip at extreme rpm. The R90S alternator was also less powerful than that of the other /6 models, providing 240 watts as opposed to 280. Unchanged from the /5 was the starter motor above the engine, and 1974 R90Ss and /6s retained the kick-start.

The most significant drivetrain development was the incorporation of a five-speed gearbox on all 1974 models. A new, lighter aluminium housing was actually smaller than the four-speed unit, and the gearbox design retained three shafts. While an improvement, the gear selection and shifting still wasn't perfect. Over the next few years there would be myriad updates to the selection mechanism, but the gearbox remained the drivetrain's weak link. The single plate dry clutch was much as before, although the R90S received a stronger diaphragm spring.

Apart from some additional gussets, the /6 frame and swingarm were similar to those of the final /5. Because the /6 (and R90S) also retained the bolt-on rear subframe, and pressed steel fork upper triple clamp, the structure still incorporated some flex. When combined with the same long travel suspension of the /5, the

resulting /6 (and R90S) were not sharp handling sportsters like some British and Italian motorcycles, but efficient long-distance sport tourers.

While the 19in and 18in wheels, with light alloy rims, and 200mm Simplex rear drum brake were the same as on the /5, new on the R75/6, R90/6, and R90S was the front brake. An ATE 38mm single piston brake caliper gripped the solid 260mm stainless steel disc on the front of the R75/6 and R90/6. To tidy the handlebar layout, and provide crash protection, the front master cylinder was located underneath the fuel tank. A Bowden cable connected the master cylinder to the handlebar lever, introducing imprecision into the system. The R90S had a dual front disc brake set-up (with larger 15.87mm master cylinder), and while this was also an option on the /6 it was an expensive proposition, as the stock right-side fork leg didn't include a brake caliper mount. The R60/6 retained the earlier front Duplex

Apart from a disc front brake, full instrumentation, and five-speed gearbox, the R75/6 was very similar to the R75/5. This 1976 model has the optional dual disc set-up. (Ian Falloon)

R90S and /6 specifications

	R60/6	R75/6	R90/6	R90S
Bore (mm)	73.5	82	90	90
Stroke (mm)	70.6	70.6	70.6	70.6
Capacity (cc)	599	745	898	898
Compression ratio	9.2:1	9.0:1	9.0:1	9.5:1
Horsepower DIN/SAE	40@6,400rpm 46@6,600rpm	50@6,200rpm 57@6,400rpm	60/6,500rpm 67/6,700rpm	67/7,000rpm 75/7,200rpm
Left carburettor	Bing 1/26/111	Bing 64/32/9	Bing 64/32/11	Dell'Orto PHM 38 BS
Right carburettor	Bing 1/26/112	Bing 64/32/10	Bing 64/32/12	Dell'Orto PHM 38 BD
Overall width	740mm (29.1in)	740mm (29.1in)	740mm (29.1in)	740mm (29.1in)
Seat height	810mm (31.9in)	810mm (31.9in)	810mm (31.9in)	830mm (32.7in)
Overall length	2,180mm (85.8in)	2,180mm (85.8in)	2,180mm (85.8in)	2,180mm (85.8in)
Wheelbase	1,465mm (57.7in)	1,465mm (57.7in)	1,465mm (57.7in)	1,465mm (57.7in)
Weight including oil but without fuel	200kg (441lb)	200kg (441lb)	200kg (441lb)	205kg (452lb)
Weight including oil and fuel	210kg (463lb)	210kg (463lb)	210kg (463lb)	215kg (474lb)
Top speed	167kph (104mph)	177kph (110mph)	188kph (117mph)	Over 200kph (124mph)

drum, while the rear drum brake on all /6s didn't incorporate the chrome cover. Instead there were brake lining wear inspection windows.

Undoubtedly the disc brake, particularly the dual disc set-up, provided an improvement over the earlier drum, but it still lacked ultimate power compared to rival Italian and British systems. The combination of floating piston caliper and remote master cylinder provided only adequate braking, and was one of the weakest areas in the performance package, particularly of the R90S. Yet, despite a few minor updates, this set-up would last until 1981.

Even more so than engine performance, the styling of the R90S set new standards for production motorcycles. While the regular /6 was virtually indistinguishable from the /5, retaining a similar fuel tank and seat design, the R90S had a beautifully finished small cockpit fairing, and a new tank and seat. The fuel tank represented the epitome of design excellence; not only did it hold a useful 24 litres, but it was beautifully sculptured. Almost graceful in its elegance, the style of the fuel tank was so successful that within three years it featured on all large capacity boxers. Even the resurrected boxers of 1985 incorporated this tank design, and it lasted until the final R100RT of 1996.

After 22 years it still didn't look out of date, and was certainly more attractive than the tank of the Paralever R100R.

The R90S also featured an individual colour scheme, hand-painted and air brushed silver smoke. Because no suitable paint was initially found to provide a uniform pinstripe finish, early R90Ss had gold tape highlighting. Only this tape and the plastic BMW tank emblems detracted from the excellent quality. Later R90Ss had hand-painted pinstripes, but the era of enamel tank badges was over.

Accompanying the new tank on the R90S was a dual seat on a fibreglass base that incorporated a sporting rear cowling, and a fibreglass handlebar-mounted fairing. This fairing was innovative for a mainstream sporting motorcycle, and incorporated plastic automotive-style padding and a clock and voltmeter. This was the first time a clock had featured on a production motorcycle since the Ariel Leader. The separate speedometer and tachometer with warning light console were mounted on the top triple clamp, and finally the plunger ignition switch disappeared, to be replaced by a key. This was still rather inconveniently located on the left headlight-mounting bracket but was a welcome change. Completing the list of improvements over the /5 was a larger (180mm/7.1in) Bosch H4 halogen headlight. The R90S also included a three-way adjustable double acting hydraulic steering damper underneath the steering head. The steering damper knob turned a shaft inside the steering head tube, moving the damper away from the steering head axis to provide an effective damping adjustment.

1974 R90Ss and /6s also included the older (/5-style) Hella handlebar switches, finger-indented Magura levers, and Magura cam and chain throttle. Unfortunately, as this throttle was designed for small throat Bing carburettors, it was extremely slow acting on the R90S with its large 38mm carburettors. This was one of the few design flaws in the thoroughly developed R90S, and was rectified for 1975.

The 1975 R90S, R90/6, R75/6, and R60/6

Only a few updates appeared on the R90S and /6 for 1975. Inside the engine were a new

crankshaft, front main bearing, and flywheel, and the kick-start at the rear of the transmission was no longer standard. The kick-start remained an option, and to ensure reliable ignition the starter motor was upgraded slightly, to 0.6bhp. Later in the model year there were new shifting forks in the gearbox. Chassis updates included a larger diameter front axle (up to 17mm from 14mm), and perforated front discs on the 900 and 750cc models. These holes were intended to improve wet weather performance. In addition the R90S received new fork dampers.

Also new for 1975 were the handlebar switches and controls. Not only were the Magura dogleg levers ergonomically superior, but the new R90S throttle assembly provided a faster action. The integrated Hella handlebar switches were much more up-to-date in looks and function than the /5 type, but remained typically idiosyncratic as they incorporated the turn signals on the right. The R90S was also available in the spectacular Daytona Orange.

Updates to the R90S for 1975 included drilled front brake discs.

The Butler & Smith R90S Superbikes

The release of the R90S for 1974 also coincided with the expansion in production, and production-based racing in America. As Reg Pridmore and the Butler & Smith R75/5 were the most competitive combination in West Coast production racing during 1973, it was no surprise to see them on the leader board with the new R90S during 1974. Pridmore was denied a win in the Production race at Laguna Seca when an ignition wire broke, but made amends at Ontario where he finished so far in front of the Yoshimura Kawasakis that they assumed they had won! As production racing evolved into AMA-sanctioned Superbike racing in the US, so did the R90S.

By 1976 two-strokes had driven four-strokes out of open class racing, but as they bore no relationship to street motorcycles the AMA created the Superbike series to woo the fans back. The rules required Superbikes to look outwardly stock, even retaining a taillight, but underneath the street bodywork were highly developed racers. In the first year of Superbike, only Butler & Smith, with their R90Ss, exploited the regulations to the full.

West Coast executives Helmut Kern and Matt Capri, team manager Udo Gietl, with Todd Schuster, Kenny Augustine, and Tom Woods, worked tirelessly to create arguably the most spectacular BMW racing motorcycles ever.

German-born but US-educated, Gietl was an electrical engineer with experience at NASA and on the Polaris submarine missile. He knew that to compete with the Kawasaki Z1 they would need as much power as possible, and went to extraordinary lengths to achieve it. 95mm forged Venolia pistons bumped the capacity to 1,000cc and provided more than 12:1 compression. Three different brands of piston ring were used, a special L-section top ring, Chevrolet middle ring, and Perfect Circle oil control ring. As the engine had to rev safely to 9,200rpm, the gudgeon pins were machined from K11 heat-treated steel. Inside the cylinder head were stainless steel 46mm inlet and 39mm exhaust valves, and Augustine flowed the cylinder heads. Schuster bored and worked the 38mm Dell'Orto carburettors to 40mm, while the camshaft was by Sig Erson and provided 12mm of intake valve lift. The shorter pushrods were chrome-molybdenum, and from Germany came very thin steel valve lifters.

In an effort to increase cornering clearance, the cylinder barrels were shortened, along with special 10mm shorter German forged titanium con-rods, and the rocker covers were bevelled and fitted with

steel skid plates. The crankshaft was stock, and Gietl fabricated an all-metal dry clutch, with the power transported through a close-ratio gearbox. Retaining the stock BMW third, fourth, and fifth gears, Augustine made up closer first and second gears. Four coils fired the twin spark plugs per cylinder, and all superfluous components (such as the electric start and air filter box) were discarded. As stock mufflers were required by the regulations, these were gutted and fitted with a reverse-cone megaphone designed by C.R. Axtel for Harley XR750s. When they lined up at the inaugural Superbike race at Daytona in March 1976, the Butler & Smith R90Ss produced 92bhp at the clutch.

Although the engine modifications continued along the trail blazed by the R75/5 and North-framed racers, Gietl took a hard look at the chassis regulations and stretched them to the limit. A loophole indicated that the swingarm could be modified, with the rear suspension relocated, so this is what B&S did. Gietl and Schuster reworked the swingarm to incorporate a single, semi-horizontal, Koni F1 racing car shock absorber. At the same time, a spacer behind the gearbox shifted the engine forward 30mm and upwards 10mm. The engine was also repositioned slightly to the right to allow clearance between the Michelin slick tyre and driveshaft. The stock BMW forks were reworked, strengthened with a huge alloy top triple clamp, and braced. Wider WM4 and WM5 18in alloy wire-spoked wheels allowed wider slick tyres, and initially the brakes were still the stock ATE floating caliper type. The weight was around 370lb (168kg).

Three machines were prepared, and Pridmore, Steve McLaughlin, and Gary Fisher lined up at Daytona. Although there were a few teething problems during practice, Fisher was timed at 144.5mph (233kph) and all three riders qualified for the

Left: The 1976 Butler & Smith Superbikes were possibly the most highly developed air-cooled boxer twins of all time, and no expense was spared in their preparation. (Bruce Armstrong)

Opposite: Steve McLaughlin on his way to victory in the 1976 Daytona Superbike race. (Mick Woollett)

final. Helmut Kern switched Pridmore's bike back to a conventional dual shock rear end, and Fisher led until a rocker arm broke. McLaughlin took over the lead but was soon caught by Pridmore. On the final lap Pridmore led, but McLaughlin drafted past across the finishing line to win by three inches. Pridmore was initially credited with victory but the photo finish equipment later proved McLaughlin the winner. It was one of the closest race finishes ever at Daytona, and the race average was 99.8mph (160kph). Pridmore went on to win two more Superbike races that year, and had the consolation of eventually winning the 1976 AMA Superbike Championship. Developments during the season saw twin-piston Lockheed brake calipers installed on

the front, and the power rise to around 100bhp at 8,200rpm. Steve McLaughlin almost destroyed the Daytona winner (number 83) in a horrendous crash at Laguna Seca.

The monoshock rear suspension was banned for 1977, and Pridmore fronted on the Butler & Smith R90S (painted red R100S colours) at Daytona with the power up by 7bhp. Pridmore finished fourth, and B&S then retired from racing. They had proven the R90S was a Superbike, and the bikes were sold to three sponsored dealers (Johnny's Motorcycle Company, San Jose BMW, and BMW Fort Worth). Ron Pierce gave the McLaughlin bike another victory, at Laguna Seca, but it was later restored to its former glory.

After B&S's retirement Gietl and Schuster prepared another R90S Superbike. Limited resources meant Gietl could only prepare one machine for the 1978 season, and he almost provided BMW with its second AMA Superbike Championship. Development saw the engine modified to improve reliability. The Venolia pistons were lighter by 50g, enabling tighter clearances, and to reduce crankcase pressure loss the breather fed into a foam-filled box through reed valves. The 45mm inlet valves were from a Chrysler Hemi V8, and, while still using bored Dell'Orto carburettors, for shorter tracks Gietl installed a 36mm intake restrictor. The

Continued overleaf

Continued from previous page

330° camshaft was by Crane, and the pushrods and steel tappets were straight out of an aftermarket automotive catalogue. The ignition was Bosch CDI, still with four coils and twin spark plugs per cylinder. Other modifications extended to a heavily milled flywheel, and the engine weighed only 115lb (52kg). As the gearbox was the cause of most retirements Gietl used a special close-ratio set from BMW.

Improving the handling was the other priority. The engine was moved forward 15mm in the frame to counteract wheel standing, and two welded struts connected the swingarm pivot to the steering head. Extra plates also strengthened the steering head, and the head angle was increased to 28.5°. The swingarm was extensively reinforced underneath, and the twin Koni shock

Now one of the most famous racing BMWs, McLaughlin's 1976 Daytona-winning bike remains a testament to the era when the BMW boxer was a class-leading Superbike. (Bruce Armstrong)

absorbers were extensively re-worked. To restrict fork travel under hard braking, Gietl incorporated a mechanical anti-dive, with each of the Lockheed brake calipers mounted on an alloy rocker arm pivoting from the front axle. Each rocker was linked by ball joint and pushrod to the lower fork crown. The twin front discs were light-weight plasma-coated aluminium. As Superbike regulations allowed a 20 per cent weight reduction from stock, Gietl's BMW weighed a significant 20kg (44lb) less than the Suzuki GS1000, and 27kg (60lb) less than the Kawasaki Z1000.

Gietl's rider for 1978 was John Long, who finished a surprising third at the opening race at Daytona. A second at Loudon, and finally a victory at Mosport, saw Long ending the season with a points tie for the AMA Superbike Championship. With only one victory, he was credited with second, but for a privately entered pushrod twin to succeed so well in a field of factory-prepared fours it was an astonishing achievement. This was the last BMW victory in an AMA Superbike event, and represented the end of the era in which the pushrod twin with power-robbing shaft drive was still a force to be reckoned with.

After Butler & Smith retired from AMA Superbike racing Udo Gietl persevered with the R90S, installing a mechanical anti-dive on the Superbike racer. John Long nearly won the 1978 AMA Superbike Championship on this machine. (Author's collection)

The author's 1976 R90S, one of the best-looking and best-performing air-cooled boxers.
(Ian Falloon)

The 1976 R90S, R90/6, R75/6, and R60/6

Although the 1976 R90S and /6 looked visually identical to those of 1975, there were a significant number of improvements, many as precursors to the 980cc /7 already under development. The engine model type was 247/76, with the crankcases reinforced to accept larger cylinder spigots. There was a deeper oil sump pan, but the sump capacity of 2.25 litres was unchanged, and the new sump moved the oil further from the crankshaft to reduce oil drag. There were also new cylinder heads, with new rocker arms and support blocks, and 20 per cent lighter, hollow aluminium and steel pushrods. Although the camshaft valve lift and timing were as before, the camshaft spindle diameter was increased from 12 to 20mm, to reduce camshaft flex and improve valve operation. Changes to the gearbox saw a strengthened gearbox housing, and a new gearshift cam plate and detent spring to improve the gearshift.

Along with the engine updates came some chassis developments. The swingarm received heavier gusseting directly in front of the rear tyre, and there were larger piston (40mm) ATE front brake calipers. Accompanying the latter was a new master cylinder with a larger (17.46mm) piston, considerably reducing hand lever pressure. The R75/6 and R90/6 also featured the 40mm brake caliper, and to accommodate this there was the third set of Boge forks in as many years. All these engine

and chassis developments rendered the 1976 R90S and /6 arguably the quintessential air-cooled boxer twins, combining the classic features of the earlier versions with the technical superiority of later examples.

By 1976 the future of the BMW motorcycle was secure, and a reorganisation within the company saw motorcycles separated from cars. Motorcycle production climbed to 28,209, and with the release of the /7-series imminent the future looked even brighter. However, with the demise of the /6, something also died within the BMW motorcycle. While the /7 was functionally superior, styling revisions and further attempts at cost cutting detracted from its classic appeal. Although the /6 remains undervalued and unappreciated, the R90S has now gained the classic status it deserves. More than just the first BMW Superbike, the R90S represented an era in which the BMW pushrod twin could fight on the race tracks and demolish a field of Japanese fours and Italian twins. It also pioneered luxury high performance sport touring, and remains one of the finest looking BMW motorcycles ever. It was the only BMW twin with large Dell'Orto 'pumper' carburettors, and the only model to include the round R68 rocker covers with sculptured 24-litre fuel tank. Although its production numbers of 17,465 don't really place the R90S in the category of a rare and endangered species, it is unquestionably the classic modern BMW motorcycle, combining aesthetic quality, contemporary performance superiority, and incredible racing prowess.

4 Rennsport revived

Although the R90S had revised the public perception of BMW motorcycles, there was room for improvement. Undeniably swift and comfortable, the R90S was immensely capable as a luxury sport touring motorcycle, but came in for some criticism regarding its high-speed stability. The handlebar-mounted fairing, with its high steering inertia, accentuated this instability, and Hans Muth was asked to create a new motorcycle with a more integrated aerodynamic fairing. The result was the R100RS, arguably more significant than even the R90S. Its RS (Rennsport) initials were employed to create an association with the magnificent RS54 racers, but it was a rather spurious connection. Underneath the distinctive large fibreglass fairing was the most powerful incarnation of the boxer yet, but it was still strongly derived from the /5. This didn't stop the R100RS creating a sensation when it was released at the Cologne Show towards the end of 1976.

The 1977 R100RS, R100S, and /7

With the R100RS, Muth designed a fairing emphasising rider protection and aerodynamic function, while contributing to motorcycle stability. Muth and von der Marwitz hired the finest facility available, the Pininfarina wind tunnel (at £2,600 a day), and the resulting fairing was claimed to reduce front wheel lift by 17.4 per cent, reduce drag by 5.4 per cent, and the yawing moment in side winds by 60 per cent. All this with a weight penalty of only 9.5kg (20.9lb). The nine-piece fairing design was so advanced that it remains a benchmark in motorcycle fairing efficiency, and few later examples can match it. But there was more to

the R100RS than an efficient fairing. The engine (Designation M65* and Type 247/76) was already updated for 1976, but featured further reinforced crankcases, and 94mm cylinders and pistons to provide 980cc. The cylinders had thicker and shorter cooling fins, to reduce noise, and were no longer painted black (as on the R90S). To cope with the increased crankcase pressure, the crankcase ventilation system was improved. There were larger (44mm) inlet valves and new angular, black anodised rocker covers with polished fins.

Instead of the concentric Dell'Orto carburettors of the R90S, the R100RS received Bing 40mm Type 94 constant-vacuum carburettors, and there were larger diameter (40mm) exhaust header pipes to provide an increase in power of the otherwise identical R100S engine. The 180mm single disc dry clutch was much the same, but with a heavier duty anti-warp clutch disc, and a thinner flywheel, although the weight of the clutch assembly was unchanged. To improve the starting ratio for the larger engine the number of teeth on the flywheel was increased to 94. The transmission case received lengthwise exterior ribbing, but the five-speed gearbox was unchanged.

Alongside the R100RS was the new /7-series. The R100S replaced the R90S (also with Bing carburettors), the R100/7 the R90/6, while the R75/7 and R60/7 were very similar to their predecessors. The engines for all the /7s incorporated the R100RS updates. The R100RS and R100S retained the smaller alternator of the R90S, but the improved starter ratio and larger 28Ah battery, assisted cold temperature starting. The kick-start was still an option. The other /7s included the 280-watt alternator of the R90/6, R75/6, and R60/6.

R100RS, R100RT, R100S, R100T, and /7 specifications (1977–80)

	R60/7	R75/7	R80/7	R100/7	R100T	R100S	R100RS	R100RT
Bore (mm)	73.5	82	84.8	94	94	94	94	94
Stroke (mm)	70.6	70.6	70.6	70.6	70.6	70.6	70.6	70.6
Capacity (cc)	599	745	797	980	980	980	980	980
Compression ratio	9.2:1	9.0:1	9.2:1	9.1:1	9.5:1	9.5:1	9.5:1	9.5:1
Horsepower DIN (from 1979)	40@ 6,400rpm	50@ 6,200rpm	55@ 7,000rpm	60@ 6,500rpm	65@ 6,600rpm	65@ 6,600rpm (70@ 7,250rpm)	70@ 7,250rpm	70@ 7,250rpm
Left carburettor	Bing 1/26/123	Bing 64/32/13	Bing 64/32/201	Bing 64/32/19	Bing 94/40/103	Bing 94/40/103	Bing 94/40/105	Bing 94/40/105
Right carburettor	Bing 1/26/124	Bing 64/32/14	Bing 64/32/202	Bing 64/32/20	Bing 94/40/104	Bing 94/40/104	Bing 94/40/106	Bing 94/40/106
Overall width	746mm (29.4in)	746mm (29.4in)	746mm (29.4in)	746mm (29.4in)	746mm (29.4in)	746mm (29.4in)	746mm (29.4in)	746mm (29.4in)
Saddle height	810mm (31.9in)	810mm (31.9in)	810mm (31.9in)	810mm (31.9in)	810mm (31.9in)	820mm (32.3in)	820mm (32.3in)	820mm (32.3in)
Overall length	2,180mm (85.8in)	2,180mm (85.8in)	2,180mm (85.8in)	2,180mm (85.8in)	2,180mm (85.8in)	2,180mm (85.8in)	2,180mm (85.8in)	2,180mm (85.8in)
Wheelbase	1,465mm (57.7in)	1,465mm (57.7in)	1,465mm (57.7in)	1,465mm (57.7in)	1,465mm (57.7in)	1,465mm (5 7.7in)	1,465mm (57.7in)	1,465mm (57.7in)
Weight including oil but without fuel	195kg (430lb)	195kg (430lb)	195kg (430lb)	195kg (430lb)	195kg (430lb)	200kg (441lb)	210kg (463lb)	215kg (472lb)
Weight including oil and fuel	215kg (474lb)	215kg (474lb)	215kg (474lb)	215kg (474lb)	215kg (474lb)	220kg (485lb)	230kg (507lb)	234kg (516lb)
Top speed	167kph (104mph)	177kph (110mph)	182kph (113mph)	188kph (117mph)	195kph (121mph)	Over 200kph (124mph)	Over 200kph (124mph)	190kph (118mph)

Although the /7 frame and swingarm were essentially unchanged from the final 1976 version, a second transverse tube was added between the front double downtubes and the frame tubing was a thicker section. The chassis type was 247/77, and included additional gusseting around the steering head. Modified front fork damping resulted in a softer ride in the middle range of fork movement. Despite these welcome improvements, the front fork still included the weak pressed steel upper triple clamp, and the rear subframe was bolted on as before. The R100RS retained the adjustable steering damper, but this no longer featured as standard equipment on the R100S.

Most 1977 R100RSs were fitted with spoked wheels with the usual aluminium rims, but included distinguishing blue pinstripes. All /7s this year also featured wire-spoked wheels, but cast-alloy 'snowflake' wheels were listed as an option for the R100RS. The rear rim width on the alloy wheels (still with a drum brake) was increased to 2.5in, and while these featured in brochures and some early magazines they weren't generally available during 1977. Undoubtedly more rigid, the cast wheels were heavier than the wire-spoked type, and prone to cracking.

Apart from the R60/7, that now included a single front disc brake, there was no change to the R100RS, R100S, and /7 front brake set-up from the twin disc 1976 R90S and single disc /6. To set the R100RS apart it had blue-anodised ATE brake calipers, and all models retained the Simplex rear drum brake.

If the R90S had stretched the sporting boundaries with its low handlebar and semi-racer riding position, the R100RS took this a step further. There was an even narrower, clip-on style handlebar that not only fitted inside the fairing but provided a very aggressive riding position. Considerable weight was placed on the wrists, encouraging high-speed touring. The combination of sporting riding position, aerodynamically efficient fairing, and improved stability, saw the R100RS the leader in sport-touring motorcycles.

The injection-moulded fibreglass R100RS fairing set the world talking. Full coverage fairings were unusual at that time, and only full touring motorcycles were so equipped. These generally provided barn door aerodynamics so the RS fairing was a functional revelation. Not only was it frame-mounted, but the headlight was moved from the front fork, further improving the steering. In front of the headlight was a Sekurit safety glass cover that incorporated five orange lines. (These were purely a styling addition, with no functional value.) The front fairing section was a grille that allowed air to the front of the engine, while the lower sections could be removed for riding in hot weather. The design of the low windshield also came in for some criticism, as it generated turbulence around the rider's helmet.

Although the R100RS instrument layout closely followed that of the R90S, the instrument set-up and warning lights were even more integrated into the fairing. The speedometer and tachometer were still mounted on the top triple clamp, and an automotive-style plastic cover concealed the handlebar. The ignition key was more conveniently located between the voltmeter and electric clock. All other /7s retained the earlier ignition location.

All /7s now featured the elegant 24-litre R90S fuel tank, but only the R100RS and R100S included the sporting seat. There was also a choice of a sporting solo, almost one-and-a-half, seat for the R100RS. The only colour available for the first R100RS was flat metallic silver.

Although the layout of the Hella handlebar switches was the same as before, the right indicator switch now included a thumb extension wing for ease of operation, as did the left high/low beam and flasher switch. The horn was much stronger than before, with twin Italian Fiamms. Located below the fuel tank, the sound

bounced off the inner fairing panels and could be disconcerting for the rider. As there was now an additional frame brace where the Bosch horn was previously located, other /7s also had a Fiamm, but only a single horn on the left.

When it was released the R100RS was one of the most expensive motorcycles available, and despite retaining a relatively unsophisticated engine it could still match any other sport-touring motorcycle. It was no longer a Superbike, but an incomparable road burner, and another classic BMW twin.

Although the R100RS supplanted the R100S at the head of the line-up, and the R100S only had a 65bhp engine, the latter was lighter and faster than both the R100RS and R90S. It was also more suited to production racing. In the Australian Castrol Six-Hour race for stock production motorcycles the R90S managed second in 1975 and 1976 behind Kawasaki Z1s, but the tables turned in 1977, when Kenny Blake and Joe Eastmure rode their R100S to victory, while Helmut Dähne and Tony Hatton finished fifth, ahead of Mike Hailwood on a Ducati 750 SS.

Early R100RSs had wire-spoked wheels and are now considered collectors' items.
(Ian Falloon)

The 1978 R100RS, R100S, and /7

There were only detail changes to the R100RS and /7 for 1978, and while the engine specifications were unchanged the camshaft timing was advanced 6°. In an effort to improve the gearshift, the gear lever now pivoted on the rider's footpeg attachment and attached to the small shifting lever with a U rod. Only the 'snowflake' cast alloy wheels were fitted to the R100RS (and soon the R100S), the rear 18in wheel featuring a wider 2.75in rim and incorporating a drilled Brembo 260mm disc brake with twin-piston brake caliper. This was a superior brake to the front swinging calipers, and seemed an anomaly.

The R80/7 replaced the R75/7, and was very similar but for 84.8mm pistons and cylinders. The engine designation was M85*. Along with the R100/7 and R60/7, the R80/7 retained the wire-spoked wheels with a rear drum brake. All models shared new instruments, with green numerals and an electronic tachometer and quartz clock. The range of colours was also expanded, with the R100RS also available in metallic gold, along with a limited edition Motorsport in white. While the range of

motorcycles was now the largest in BMW's history, there was unease as the strong German currency continued to force up prices in the strongest export market, the United States. During 1977 and 1978 sales diminished, and it was rumoured that up to 8,000 motorcycles sat in dealers' showrooms. US sales of the flagship R100RS diminished to only 1,092 in 1978.

In response to this crisis virtually the entire management team was replaced at the end of 1978, but there were other difficulties facing the venerable boxer twin. Noise, emission controls, and the introduction of lower octane low lead fuel were hurting the engine. US models also required complicated engine breather set-ups. In the face of cheaper and higher performing Japanese fours, the expensive boxers struggled to find a market in the US, although they continued to maintain a loyal following in Europe.

The 1979 R100RS, R100RT, R100S, R100T, and /7

Supplanting the R100RS in the 1979 line-up, with the highest price and most equipment, was the full touring R100RT. Although its life began

Opposite: The R100S replaced the R90S from 1977, and the 1979 version shown here featured cast alloy wheels and a rear disc brake. (Ian Falloon)

New for 1979 was the R100RT. This wasn't initially very popular, but eventually became one of the most successful air-cooled boxers. (Ian Falloon)

precariously, as it was aimed at the fickle US market, the R100RT ultimately established a formula that was more successful than the R100RS. It lasted through until 1996, and even today the R1150RT comfortably outsells the R1150RS.

Shared with all 1979 boxers were the most significant engine revisions since the first /5 of 1970. There was a new crankshaft, now with riveted counterweights, and during the model year O-rings were incorporated at the base of each cylinder for improved sealing. The camshaft drive was now by a single row chain, incorporating a spring-loaded hydraulically damped tensioner, and there was a new automotive-style ignition. Although retaining a Bosch contact breaker, a rotary trigger was enclosed in a housing within the timing chain cover. The points cam was driven off the end of the camshaft via a self aligning floating tang and groove Oldham coupling, and was claimed to isolate the points from camshaft flex and vibration. Completing the engine updates was a new alternator cover and chain case, and a double-sided engine breather. The R100RS now included a standard oil cooler.

To further assist gear disengagement the driveshaft incorporated a torsional vibrator. This consisted of an additional ramped coupling and spring, similar to that on the transmission input shaft, and was the most effective modification to the gearshift up to that time. The transmission case also received external vertical cross ribbing for additional strength and heat dissipation.

The year saw some engine rationalisation, with the R100RT and R100S sharing the 70bhp engine of the R100RS. The previous 65bhp R100S engine (still with 40mm Bing carburettors) went to power the R100T. All the 980cc engines now had 44mm inlet and 40mm exhaust valves.

Chassis changes were minimal, and all models now included reflectors on the fork legs. While the R100RS bodywork was as before, the inclusion of an oil cooler saw a new solid centre lower fairing panel. As it got very hot under this panel, there was occasional diode board failure. A dual seat was now standard, with a larger black passenger grab rail that included a rack, while the solo seat remained an option. In addition to metallic gold, there was now a two-tone blue silver metallic finish with red

pinstriping. This was definitely one of the most attractive colour schemes offered for the RS.

Expanding on the RS integral cockpit concept, the R100RT fairing was also perfected in a wind tunnel. Even with the high and wide handlebar, the frame-mounted fairing provided hand protection, and the high windshield was manually adjustable for three rake and height positions. Air intakes under the turn indicators channelled air into the fairing through automotive style adjustable air vents with a butterfly valve. Carried over from the R100RS was the headlight cover with the same strange five orange lines. The instrument panel was similar to that of the R100RS, with room for additional switches and control lamps for the wide range of optional extras. Initially these included long distance headlamps and fog lamps, and later flip-out driving lights in place of the air vents. The fairing also included two six-litre lockable storage compartments beneath the air vents. The R100RT came with luggage racks for the standard lockable Krauser saddlebags, and shared with the R100RS were the steering damper and twin Fiamm horns.

Setting the R100RT apart from the R100RS were cast wheels painted a hue of light Phoenix gold, and very 1970s colours of two-tone brown with Phoenix gold. The other colour was smoke red, with silver wheels. Although it was well finished, and outfitted with considerable standard equipment, the high price and moderate performance counted against the R100RT in America. The release of the smaller R65 hastened the demise of the R60/7, and to fill a void between the R100S and R100/7 there was a new model for 1979, the R100T. R100T specification varied depending on the country, but often included chrome saddlebag brackets and engine protection bars, and additional instrumentation.

Completing the 1979 upgrades were new handlebar switches, with a more conventional left-side turn signal switch. No fork gaiters were now fitted to any models, and while only cast alloy wheels were specified, the R100T, R100/7, and R80/7 retained the rear disc brake (with slightly narrower 2.5in rim). Twin front disc brakes were also now standard. The seat for the R100T, R100/7, and R80/7 was the same type as on the R100S, with a fibreglass base and tail.

With 24,415 motorcycles manufactured during 1979, production was the lowest since

1974. In an effort to stem this downward spiral, an R100RS was prepared for an attempt on a series of long distance records. In October 1979, at Nardo in Italy, a team of four riders (Dähne, Cosutti, Milan, and Zanini) set five new world records, including an average speed of 220.711kph (137.061mph) over 100km. The lowered R100RS was only lightly modified.

The 1980 R100RS, R100RT, R100S, R100T, and /7

Because most developmental resources were now directed towards the new K-series and G/S, the 1980 /7 models were ostensibly identical to those of 1979. There were some evolutionary developments, however, including a modification to the lubrication system to improve oil flow to the rear main bearing. All US versions featured lower compression (8.2:1) pistons and 38mm exhaust header pipes, with a consequent lowering of claimed power to 67bhp at 7,000rpm. US models also received a redesigned sand-cast aluminium air-filter box, with a flat air filter, and twin snorkel air intakes. This was identical in design to the plastic airbox that would appear for 1981. There was a revised crankcase ventilation system, and two tubes connecting the air filter box to each exhaust port in the cylinder head. This Pulse-Air suction emission system included a one-way reed valve in the airbox, and endeavoured to reduce the level of un-burnt hydrocarbons by mixing the exhaust gases with clean air. There was an unfortunate side effect of popping in throttle off deceleration. US models also included a relocation of the choke lever from the air filter box to the clutch lever bracket on the handlebar. This was because there was no longer room on the new air filter box.

As the price continued to climb in America, and the performance diminished, sales stagnated to such an extent that only 3,866 1,000cc models were sold in the US during 1979 and 1980. This led to a change in US distribution, and in October 1980 BMW North America took over from Butler & Smith. A limited edition R100S 'Exclusive Sport' was also offered for 1980. Painted metallic silver with triple-tone blue striping, this also featured polished fork legs, rocker covers and final drive housing. The cast wheels were also a matching light silver, but

there was a much more significant series of developments in store for 1981.

The 1981–84 R100RS, R100RT, R100CS, R100, and R80RT

Despite the impending release of the K100, destined to replace the larger capacity boxer, the R-series received significant updates for 1981. These revisions would see the venerable boxer through until 1984, and this series epitomised the finest attributes of the air-cooled boxer. Some of the elegant features of the earlier boxers were lost, but the improvements to the drivetrain and chassis were more valuable. The line-up was rationalised, with the R100RS, R100RT, and R100CS (replacing the R100S) receiving the same 70bhp engine. The R100 replaced the R100T and R100/7, while the R80/7 continued as before, with the 1981 updates, but was primarily produced for police duties. All US versions also featured the lower compression 67bhp R100 engine.

Engine developments (designation A10) included a deeper sump and Nikasil (by Mahle) or Galnikal (by Kolben Schmidt) cylinders. Extremely hard-wearing silicon-carbide was applied directly to the aluminium cylinders, improving heat dissipation and saving weight. Experience with the smaller R65 had shown the benefits of a lighter clutch and flywheel,

The R100RT cockpit was similar to the R100RS but more expansive. This is a 1981 model, but all were very similar. (Ian Falloon)

Many updates were incorporated from 1981, including Brembo front brakes and electronic ignition, but the style of the R100RS was unchanged. (Ian Falloon)

Opposite: The R100RT at the 1981 press launch in Morocco. (Mick Woollett)

especially in combination with the driveshaft shock absorber, and this was passed onto the new engine. There was a new thinner and smaller diameter (165mm) clutch, with much stronger diaphragm spring, and spring plate. Along with a substantially lighter pressed steel (rather than billet cast) flywheel, a three-spoked cross with riveted ring starter gear, the weight of the flywheel and clutch assembly was reduced by 40 per cent, with a resulting improvement in throttle response. The new clutch featured a revised operating mechanism, with a 30 per cent reduction in lever effort.

Along with a revised double-sided crankcase breather, there were new cylinder heads, with exhaust valve seats suitable for low lead fuel. There were minor updates to the 40mm Bing carburettors, but the biggest development was the incorporation of a new airbox and flat rectangular air filter as featured on 1980 US models. Instead of cast aluminium, the airbox was black plastic, with two removable forward-facing plastic snorkels. The smoother plastic finish was claimed to reduce turbulence and restriction, permitting leaner jetting, but it was also undoubtedly cheaper to produce. One

benefit, though, was vastly improved air filter access, even if the plastic looked rather cheap compared to the earlier aluminium cover. US versions retained the twin exhaust air intake pipes, but now incorporated a vacuum shut-off connected to the reed valve inside the airbox. The R100RS retained an oil cooler, but this still didn't feature on other R100s.

As with 1980 US models, the choke lever was relocated to the left handlebar clutch assembly, and while the Magura throttle assembly retained the excellent cam and chain system there was now a single cable connecting to a junction block, with two cables running to each carburettor. This was claimed to reduce friction. Modifications to the exhaust system saw a return to 38mm exhaust header pipes, and an additional rear crossover balance pipe behind the sump to help broaden the powerband. Another significant improvement was the incorporation of Bosch TSZH electronic ignition. This breakerless system used a Hall effect trigger with integral centrifugal advance. All R100s, including the R100RS, now featured the more powerful Bosch 280-watt alternator.

R100RS, R100RT, R100CS, R100, and R80RT *specifications (1981–4)*

	R80RT	R100	R100CS	R100RS	R100RT
Bore (mm)	84.8	94	94	94	94
Stroke (mm)	70.6	70.6	70.6	70.6	70.6
Capacity (cc)	797	980	980	980	980
Compression ratio	8.2:1	8.2:1	9.5:1	9.5:1	9.5:1
Horsepower DIN	50@6,500rpm	67@7,000rpm	70@7,000rpm	70@7,000rpm	70@7,000rpm
Left carburettor	Bing 64/32/305	Bing 94/40/111	Bing 94/40/111	Bing 94/40/111	Bing 94/40/111
Right carburettor	Bing 64/32/306	Bing 94/40/112	Bing 94/40/112	Bing 94/40/112	Bing 94/40/112
Overall width	746mm (29.4in)	746mm (29.4in)	746mm (29.4in)	746mm (29.4in)	746mm (29.4in)
Seat height	820mm (32.3in)	820mm (32.3in)	820mm (32.3in)	820mm (32.3in)	820mm (32.3in)
Overall length	2,210mm (87.0in)	2,210mm (87.0in)	2,210mm (87.0in)	2,210mm (87.0in)	2,210mm (87.0in)
Wheelbase	1,465mm (57.7in)	1,465mm (57.7in)	1,465mm (57.7in)	1,465mm (57.7in)	1,465mm (57.7in)
Weight including oil but without fuel	214kg (471lb)	199kg (437lb)	200kg (441lb)	210kg (463lb)	217kg (478lb)
Weight including oil and fuel	235kg (518lb)	218kg (481lb)	220kg (485lb)	230kg (507lb)	237kg (522lb)
Top speed	161kph (100mph)	170kph (106mph)	190kph (118mph)	Over 200kph (124mph)	190kph (118mph)

Although the basic design of the five-speed gearbox was unchanged, inside the transmission housing were a new mainshaft, drive pinion and seal, and input shaft. The rear final drive casting was a lighter and stronger pressure die casting, similar to that of the new monoshock R80 G/S. There were also a few subtle changes to the frame and swingarm. A new rear subframe improved battery access, and the swingarm, with an additional cylindrical tube, was stiffer.

Although the cast aluminium 'snowflake' wheels looked similar to before, the front wheel was now a wider 2.15 x 19in. While retaining the same travel and leading axle, the Sachs-built front fork was also new, with modified damping, and each fork leg was cast to accept a rectangular reflector. The fork legs also accepted twin 38mm piston Brembo brake calipers, with asbestos-free pads. While the perforated disc diameter remained a relatively small 260mm, the Brembo calipers, combined with the relocation of the Magura front brake master cylinder to the handlebar, provided vastly improved braking performance. Wet weather braking was claimed to be 40 per cent improved. Of all the 1981 updates, those to the front brakes were probably the most welcome.

Until 1981, the braking was always marginal, especially for the higher performance 900 and 1,000cc twins. Other practical improvements extended to a manually, rather than self-retracting, side stand, and new footpeg mounts to reduce vibration.

Specific for the R100RT were new self-levelling Boge Nivomat shock absorbers. Incorporating a high-pressure oil/gas chamber in the lower part of the body, with a low-pressure chamber in the top, repeated shock absorber action saw oil transferred from the top to the lower chamber, with the shock eventually settling at a point determined by the controlling orifice in the central pumping rod. Although the spring travel was reduced to 85.5mm (3.37in), this was extremely effective, and the Nivomat was the most advanced suspension available for a touring motorcycle in 1981. All other R100s featured the earlier Boge shock absorbers, with the Nivomats an option.

As the basic bodywork remained unchanged, all the 1981 R100s looked very similar to their predecessors. Most R100RSs were smoke black or red, without pinstripes, with a John Player Special edition also available. Released to coincide with the racing 6-series JPS cars, this was black with gold wheels and decals. The fairing of the R100RT included a closed off centre section, and a windshield that provided less distortion. Replacing the R100S was the R100CS, the last descendant of the R90S. Some R100CS examples also featured a return to the traditional wire-spoked wheels of the pre-1978 era. Although the R100RS and R100RT retained a Brembo rear disc brake and wider 2.75 x 18in wheel, all R100CSs and R100s included a rear drum brake. The cast wheel was 2.50 x 18in, while the wire-spoked type was a narrower 2.15 x 18in.

In 1982, the R80RT joined the R100RT. In an effort to overcome stagnating R100RT sales, this was an almost identical motorcycle but with the R80/7 engine, a rear drum brake, and without standard luggage or Nivomat rear suspension. Although the performance was extremely leisurely, the R80RT was popular, and when the revised boxers were offered in

1984 the R80RT survived. It wasn't until 1987 that the R100RT would make a return.

Most updates to the larger boxer twins occurred for the 1981 model year, and the release of the K100 was imminent. As a result the R100 and R80 received few modifications through until 1984. For 1982 there was a new frame and centrestand, while the gearbox included revised helical input gears and fifth gear. Further gearbox modifications occurred for 1983, with an improved gear selector camplate, including deepened detent valleys to eliminate false neutrals.

With the K100-series about to supplant the R100, 1984 saw two final R100RS limited editions. A numbered Series 500 in blue and silver, with matching silver panniers, was available outside America. On the side of the fairing was a small numbered plaque, and the seat was thicker, with new upholstery. The United States received instead 250 final editions

With its wire-spoked wheels, the R100CS was reminiscent of the earlier R90S. (Ian Falloon)

in white. These had red and blue pinstripes, panniers, and came standard with single and dual seats and a BMW System II helmet. These two series were intended to be the end of the line for the R100RS, but pressure from enthusiasts saw it resurrected only two years later in Monolever form.

The new four-cylinder K100 was technologically and functionally superior, but as it lacked the charisma of the boxer it wasn't greeted as enthusiastically as expected. The K100 chassis was more rigid, and the handling superior, but the four-cylinder engine vibrated disconcertingly and lacked character. Not only was the engine bland, with the new technology came more weight, and the K100RS weighed in at a considerable 249kg (549lb) with a full tank of fuel. Its fairing was also less effective in providing protection than that of the R100RS. But the resurrected R100RS and R100RT, with less power and awkward styling, failed to revive the spirit of the pre-1984 boxer. With the demise of the twin-shock R100 and R80 came the end of one of BMW's finest series.

One of the improved features from 1981 was the Brembo front braking system. All R100RSs from 1979 also had an oil cooler. (Ian Falloon)

Opposite: Only a few R100RTs were fitted with optional driving lights. (Ian Falloon)

The final R100RS with the higher output engine was the Series 500 of 1984. This came with matching silver panniers. (Ian Falloon)

5 Lost causes

Introduced primarily for the 27bhp insurance category in Germany, the R45 was popular in that market but perceived as quite underpowered elsewhere. (BMW Mobile Tradition)

Following the discontinuation of the R50/5 at the end of 1973, BMW was left without a small capacity, entry-level motorcycle. The R60/6 and R60/7 never managed to fill this void because they were still relatively expensive, and they were generally bypassed in favour of the similar 750 or 800cc versions. Therefore when the insurance class in Germany was reorganised with favourable lower rates for motorcycles of less than 27bhp, BMW was caught without a

suitable model. The R60/7 was already underpowered, so it would have been ludicrous to offer it with only 27bhp. Instead the company responded with a new smaller series, the R45 and R65. Unfortunately, production costs for the smaller twins proved similar to those of their larger brethren, and consequently throughout their lifespan they struggled to provide value in a competitive middleweight market. Despite this impediment, the R45

proved popular in Germany in 27bhp form; the R65, however, although heavily promoted, never reached expected sales targets.

The 1979–80 R65 and R45

First displayed in June 1978, the R45 and R65 pioneered many of the updates that also appeared on the larger twins for 1979. The engines (M76* and M84*) included the single row camchain with oil-damped tensioner, O-rings at the base of the cylinders, and ignition points in a separate housing. The smaller twins also featured the spring-loaded driveshaft damper, but had a lighter flywheel and smaller diameter (160mm) clutch. As a result, the throttle response was superior to the larger models. Although the crankcases and five-speed gearbox were also shared, the R45 and R65 engine featured a shorter (61.5mm) stroke. This allowed for shorter cylinders, con-rods, and pistons, with overall engine width reduced by 560mm (2.6in), and a consequent improvement in cornering clearance.

Also essentially the same were the cylinder heads, but with smaller valves. The R65 had 38mm inlet and 34mm exhaust valves, while the R45 had 34 and 32mm valves. Because of the transfer angle with shorter cylinders, the pushrods were inside a hollow cam follower contacting the lower base instead of at the top as on the larger twins. For 1979, all R65s and R45s (apart from the 27bhp versions) had a 9.5:1 compression ratio, but this was reduced on US R65 models to 8.2:1 for 1980. Vibration was also a problem on the R65, particularly in top gear at around 55mph (88kph), the recently introduced speed limit in America. This did little to endear the expensive R65 to US buyers, who already perceived it as underpowered.

Although similar to the chassis of the /7 twins, retaining a similar duplex design with bolted on rear subframe, the R45/R65 frame backbone was a single tube and the downtubes were no longer oval in section. In addition the swingarm was 50mm (1.9in) shorter, and contributed to a shorter wheelbase. Also aiding the shorter wheelbase were 36mm centre-axle forks, which provided less travel than those of the /7 (175mm/6.8in). The forged aluminium top triple clamp was a welcome improvement, and the rear shock absorbers provided less travel (110mm/4.33in). Completing the more sporting aspect was a 1.85 x 18in cast 'snowflake' design front wheel, with a similar

18in on the rear. These now incorporated CP safety profiles to prevent the tyre slipping off the rim should it burst. There was a single 260mm front disc, with provision for a second disc, and the brake caliper was a dual piston ATE. The usual rod-operated Simplex drum brake was at the rear, and the front brake master cylinder was now on the handlebar as there was no longer room under the fuel tank. Many of the electrical components were located on the frame backbone instead of the headlight shell. Considering the R45 and R65 were produced as budget models, some of the improved specification over the /7 (such as dual piston brake calipers) was surprising.

Hans Muth designed the new angular 22-litre fuel tank. It was an attractive design but didn't rival the elegance of the /7 tank. Although the Bosch headlamp was smaller in diameter at 160mm (6.3in), the instruments were larger (100mm/3.9in) and were incorporated in a more modern plastic console. On the road, the R65 and R45 provided considerably sharper handling than their larger brothers. The combination of shorter wheelbase, less suspension travel, and increased cornering clearance contributed to the smaller twins' excellent roadholding. Unfortunately, as the weight wasn't significantly

R45 and R65
specifications (1979–80)

	R45	R65
Bore (mm)	70	82
Stroke (mm)	61.5	61.5
Capacity (cc)	473	650
Horsepower (DIN)	35(27)@7,250(6,500)rpm	45@7,250rpm
Compression ratio	9.2:1 (8.2:1)	9.2:1
Carburettors	Bing 64/28/303-304 (64/26/303-304)	Bing 64/32/2030-2040
Overall width	688mm (27.1in)	688mm (27.1in)
Overall length	2,110mm (83.1in)	2,110mm (83.1in)
Wheelbase	1,400mm (55.1in)	1,400mm (55.1in)
Weight including oil but without fuel	185kg (408lb)	185kg (408lb)
Weight including oil and fuel	205kg (452lb)	205kg (452lb)
Top speed	160kph (99mph)	175kph (109mph)

R45, R65, and R65LS
specifications (1981–4)

	R45	R65/R65LS
Bore (mm)	70	82
Stroke (mm)	61.5	61.5
Capacity (cc)	473	650
Horsepower (DIN)	35(27)@7,250rpm	50@7,250rpm
Compression ratio	9.2:1 (8.2:1)	9.2:1 (8.2:1)
Carburettors	Bing 64/28/303-304 (64/26/303-304)	Bing 64/32/307-308
Overall width	688mm (27.1in)	688mm (27.1in)
Overall length	2,110mm (83.1in)	2,110mm (83.1in)
Wheelbase	1,400mm (55.1in)	1,400mm (55.1in)
Weight including oil but without fuel	185kg (408lb)	185kg (408lb)
Weight including oil and fuel	205kg (452lb)	205kg (452lb)
Top speed	160kph (99mph)	175kph (109mph)

less than that of the 1,000cc twins, the performance was barely adequate, and the R45 was particularly slow. You really had to desperately want a BMW twin to buy one.

The R45, R65, and R65LS, 1981–4

Some amends were made to improve the power output of the R65 when revised versions were offered for 1981. Inside the engine (designation A20) were larger (40 and 36mm) valves and the power was up marginally, to 50bhp. The developments to the larger twins also made it to the R45 and R65, and included Nikasil cylinders, lighter clutch and flywheel, electronic ignition, and a larger sump. O-ring grooves were now machined in the bases of the cylinders, and there was an additional crossover pipe in the exhaust to broaden the powerband. Apart from revised steering geometry, and a stronger 10mm longer swingarm, constructed of larger diameter tubing with additional gusseting, the general chassis layout was unchanged. There was a lighter pressure die-cast final drive housing, and

Although significantly updated and improved for 1981, the smaller boxers still failed to win affection. (BMW Mobile Tradition)

for some markets a dual disc front end was standard on the R65. All these improvements contributed to making the R65 in particular an extremely competent middleweight, but compared to the latest Japanese offerings it was still expensive and underpowered.

In an effort to provide a more sporting image, the R65 was given to Hans Muth, and the result was the R65LS that appeared late in 1981. Underneath the radical styling was a stock R65, but the R65LS incorporated some unique features. While combining the instrument nacelle and headlight, the fork-mounted spoiler was claimed to reduce front-end lift by 30 per cent. Complementing this nosepiece was a new seat, with moulded passenger grab rails and increased storage capacity. Sporting features extended to the fibreglass front mudguard and lower handlebars. The styling was accentuated black, including the handlebars and flat black plasma-sprayed exhaust system. This may have looked racy, but it was poorly finished and not particularly durable. The ostentatious style extended to garish red, with white wheels, or silver colours.

The R65LS wheels were new, having been jointly developed with Alusuisse to provide the elasticity of wire-spoked wheels with the rigidity of cast wheels. The cast aluminium rim was hardened through heat-treating, with a pressure-cast star-shaped hub and curved spokes to provide some elasticity. This composite set-up not only provided the advantages of both wire-spoked and cast wheels, but made them lighter than the 'snowflake' type. The rear wheel also included a slightly larger (220mm) rod-operated Simplex rear brake. Still 18in front and rear, the front rim was a wider 2.15in, and this wheel design eventually featured on the K-series and post-1984 boxer twins. The R65LS also included twin Brembo front disc brakes.

This radical makeover did little to endear the R65LS to BMW traditionalists. For many it was ugly, and as its performance was only the same as the R65 it found few friends. It was certainly not one of Muth's better efforts, and hasn't earned the classic status of his R90S or R100RS. Although 6,389 R65LSs were produced through until 1985, as with the R45 and R65, the R65LS is one of the forgotten boxer twins. They were unloved when they were new, and they remain so today.

Designed to impart a sporting image to the staid R65, the R65LS wasn't entirely successful, and the styling hasn't stood the test of time. (Ian Falloon)

6 Gelände Strasse

Opposite: Laszlo Peres rode a prototype GS80 to second place in the 1978 German off-road championship. (BMW Mobile Tradition)

Below: With the R80 G/S BMW established a new niche market that ultimately became one of its most successful. (Ian Falloon)

While Helmut Dähne was showing that the new /5-series was suitable for production racing, Herbert Schek proved it could also be adapted for off-road competition. On a modified R75/5, he won the over 500cc German off-road championship three times in succession between 1970 and 1972. Helmut Scheer also rode an R75/5 in the 1970 ISDT, winning a silver medal, while Schek and Kurt Distler rode in the 1971

ISDT at the Isle of Man. Schek won a gold, and Distler almost won a silver before crashing on the final day. Three special R75/5-based machines were entered in the 1973 ISDT, held in America. Running self-generating CDI ignition, 32mm slide-type Bing carburettors, and shorter con-rods and cylinders, the four-speed 750cc machines produced 57bhp at 6,400rpm. There were 21 and 18in wheels, a

R80 G/S and R80ST
specifications (1981–7)

	R80 G/S	R80ST
Bore (mm)	84.8	84.8
Stroke (mm)	70.6	70.6
Capacity (cc)	797	797
Compression ratio	8.2:1	8.2:1
Horsepower DIN	50@6,500rpm	50@6,500rpm
Left carburettor	Bing V64/32/305	Bing V64/32/305
Right carburettor	Bing V64/32/306	Bing V64/32/306
Overall width	746mm (29.37in)	746mm (29.37in)
Seat height	860mm (33.9in)	845mm (33.3in)
Overall length	2,230mm (87.8in)	2,180mm (85.8in)
Wheelbase	1,465mm (57.7in)	1,446mm (56.9in)
Weight including oil but without fuel	167kg (368lb); 173kg (381lb) with electric start	183kg (403.5lb)
Weight including oil and fuel	186kg (410lb); 192kg (423lb) with electric start	198kg (437lb)
Top speed	168kph (104mph)	174kph (108mph)

shorter 1,424mm (55.5in) wheelbase, and the ISDT machines weighed 135kg (298lb) with a full tank of fuel. Schek won another gold medal, but the two-stroke Maico subsequently outclassed the four-stroke twin.

The introduction of a 750cc and above class in 1978 reopened the door for the BMW twin. For the German championship, Laszlo Peres prepared a special 800cc off-road machine, managing second. This encouraged an official return to off-road racing, and for 1979 BMW produced the GS80. This was a specialised competition model, with a 95 x 61.5mm bore and stroke, displacing 872cc. With 32mm Bing carburettors, and a 9.5:1 compression ratio, the engine produced 57bhp. There was a duplex frame, Maico forks and front brake, and monoshock rear suspension. The wheels were a 21in front and 17in rear, and the GS80 weighed 140kg (308lb). Dietmar Beinhauer managed a six-man team for the 1979 German and European enduro championships. The riders were Schek, Peres, Kurt Fischer, Rolf Witthöft, and Richard Schalber, while Fritz Witzel rode the GS80 in the ISDT at Neunkirchen/Siegerland. Schalber won the German

championship and came third in the European championship, while Witzel won his class in the ISDT. Results were even better in 1980. Werner Schütz won the German championship, Witthöft the European championship and a silver trophy in the ISDT. There was no official BMW entry in the 1981 event, as the company decided to concentrate on the Paris-Dakar rally.

While the factory team was proving the capability of the boxer twin in off-road competition, work was also progressing on a production dual-purpose model. When new management was appointed at the beginning of 1979, it sanctioned the development of two new models. One was the K-series, intended to replace the R100, while the other was an enduro boxer, designed to supplement the existing range. With limited developmental time available, the enduro intentionally drew on existing designs. Rüdiger Gutsche was appointed to head the project, and as Gutsche was an ISDT veteran on his own special R75/5-based enduro this undoubtedly sped the development. Only 21 months after the project got the go-ahead, the R80 G/S was presented at the official press launch at Avignon in the south of France. It was so successful during its first two years of production that it was the only boxer twin to survive the advent of the K-series unscathed, going on to form the basis of the final series of air-cooled twins.

The R80 G/S

As the success of the factory off-road racers was well publicised, the release of an enduro boxer wasn't totally unexpected. And while the production version wasn't expected to be a clone of the special lightweight GS80, its eventual specification was surprising. As the largest capacity dual-purpose motorcycle available at that time was the Yamaha XT500, the R80 G/S was unique. Continuing the usual BMW path of evolutionary development, the R80 G/S took the R80/7 engine, the R65 chassis, mixed them with a few individual ingredients, and the result was an innovative machine that excelled in its intended role.

G/S stood for *Gelände Strasse*, or woods/street, and the R80 G/S pioneered a new class of motorcycle, the all-purpose large capacity leisure machine. This was immediately successful and initiated a path that serves BMW well today

with the R1150GS and Adventurer. Aimed at the explorer or adventurer rider, for a dirt bike the R80 G/S was big and heavy, but for a street motorcycle its weight and size were moderate.

The R80 G/S's engine specifications were similar to the R80/7. While the power output remained the same, the high-rise 38mm two-into-one matt black exhaust system, with twin header pipes feeding into a pre-muffler and a high muffler on the left, contributed to slightly less torque at higher rpm (41.8ft/lb at 5,000rpm compared to 43.5ft/lb at 3,500rpm). Developments extended to the strengthened crankcases, Nikasil or Galnikal cylinders, Bosch TSZH electronic ignition with a micro-element voltage regulator, 10lb (4.5kg) lighter clutch and flywheel, and a plastic airbox with flat air filter. It also included a smaller sump than the other 1981 twins, and a sump protector. For 1981, starting was by kick only, and there was a new pressure die-cast final drive housing.

Shared with the R100 was the 280-watt alternator, while powering the electrical system was a much smaller 9Ah battery. Electric start

was an option, and included a 0.7-kilowatt Bosch starter motor, and a larger 16Ah battery. As with the R65, many of the electrical components were located on the right-side of the frame backbone tube. The frame was also similar to that of the R65, without any additional backbone strengthening tube. New was the bolted-on rear subframe Monolever single-sided swingarm. Also incorporating the driveshaft, the Monolever was claimed to provide 50 per cent greater torsional rigidity while weighing 2kg (4.4lb) less than the normal double-sided type.

The 36mm front fork was similar in internal design to that of the R65, but was a leading axle type with provision for dual disc brakes. The fork travel was the same 200mm (7.9in) as the larger twins, and the rear suspension was a single Boge shock absorber, providing 170mm (6.69in) of travel. As this attached at the junction of the main frame and rear subframe the rear structure was more rigid than that of the twin shock examples, with a consequent improvement in handling. The rear wheel was

The R80 G/S at the press launch in Morocco, 1981. (Mick Woollett)

75

The Paris-Dakar rally

The first Paris-Dakar was staged in 1979, and it was soon established as the world's toughest rally and premier long distance race. Run in January from the French capital to Senegal on the West African coast, the route encompassed 9,500km (5,900 miles), of which only 30 per cent was on sealed roads. For the original Paris-Dakar rally, veteran BMW off-road rider Herbert Schek prepared a special machine for French journalist and rider Jean Claude Morellet, better known as Fenouil. A crash whilst in third position forced Fenouil's retirement, but he was back for 1980, along with Hubert Auriol. With the support of BMW France, Schek again prepared special machines, but the single-cylinder Yamaha XT500s overwhelmed them.

For the 1981 event, BMW France made a more concerted effort. HPN Motorradtechnik, a small tuning firm in Seibersdorf in southern Bavaria, prepared three machines. This year, 1979 second place finisher Bernhard Neimer joined Auriol and Fenouil, while Schek entered as a privateer on his own machine. The R80 G/S-based racers had a strengthened chassis, long-range fuel tanks, and Marzocchi forks, and were supported by an impressive back-up squad that was well prepared for any emergency. Hubert Auriol rode to an easy victory, three hours in front of the second-placed Yamaha, while Fenouil came fourth and Neimer seventh. Although Schek crashed, breaking his pelvis, it was an astounding victory for BMW France.

BMW was back again in 1982, again with three entrants. Raymond Loizeaux replaced Neimer, but this year the team was plagued with mechanical problems. BMW's racing manager Dietmar Beinhauer withdrew the team during the event, but was back for 1983, when there were four official entries, the diminutive three-time World Motocross Champion Gaston Rahier joining the team. The engines displaced 1,015cc (95.5 x 70.6mm), had Bing 40mm carburettors, and produced 75bhp, although Rahier's was rumoured to produce 90bhp. The frame included a longer double-sided swingarm (to counteract the interference of engine torque reaction with suspension action), with twin Öhlins shock absorbers, along with a Maico 42mm front fork. There was a single front Brembo 280mm disc, and the weight of the 200kph (125mph) desert racers was 170kg (375lb).

Auriol won again, while Fenouil finished ninth.

For the 1984 event the BMW Paris-Dakar machines were an evolutionary development of the 1983 model. The front fork was now Marzocchi, with a smaller 260mm front disc brake, while the dual shock swingarm with Öhlins shock absorbers was retained. A huge 58-litre (12.7gal) Kevlar fuel tank dominated the machine, and while the dry weight was 175kg (386lb), fully fuelled the 1,000cc twins weighed an intimidating 250kg (551lb). The wheelbase was a gigantic 1,660mm (65.4in), and somehow the 5ft 4in (1.62m) Rahier managed to straddle the 1,030mm (40in) seat height. This year the three bike team was sponsored by Penthouse, and the BMWs were totally dominant. Rahier won, finishing 20 minutes ahead of Auriol, while Loizeaux came fifth.

Auriol switched to Cagiva for 1985, with Eddy Hau replacing him. Now with Marlboro and Playboy sponsorship, the HPN-prepared machines were similar to the previous year, but featured slightly smaller 94mm Mahle pistons and produced 70bhp at 6,500rpm. Retained was the Marzocchi fork, while twin White Power shock absorbers controlled the rear end. The fuel capacity went up to 60 litres (13.2gal), and the weight was 229kg (505lb) fully fuelled. Both Lau and Loizeaux retired early, but despite being involved in a collision with a car Rahier managed to win his second Paris-Dakar rally.

BMW was back with the same team, with Marlboro and Elf sponsorship, for 1986, but the twin's glory days were over. The GS 1000 was largely unchanged, the engine displacing 1,040cc, with 97mm 8.5:1 pistons. The power was still around 70bhp. The suspension was by Marzocchi M1 front forks and twin White Power rear shock absorbers, and a plastic shroud protected the front 260mm disc. The wheelbase was 1,600mm (62.4in), and the dry weight 169.6kg (374lb). Fuel capacity

After two victories in the Paris-Dakar race, an evolutionary R80 G/S-based racer provided BMW with another win in the 1984 event. This featured a long swingarm with twin shock absorbers. (BMW Mobile Tradition)

was 63 litres (13.8gal), and the wet weight 230kg (507lb).

Two crashes, and problems with fuel and back-up, saw Rahier finish a disappointing 14th, and Hau was the top BMW finisher in eighth. Disillusioned, Rahier quit the team, and following the death of rally promoter Thierry Sabine in a helicopter accident BMW withdrew from official competition. HPN nevertheless continued to develop Paris-Dakar machines for privateers, for whom a 1,000cc HPN R80 G/S was available during 1987. Based on the R80 G/S, but with a Marzocchi fork and twin White Power shock absorbers, the HPN desert racer was good enough to provide Hau with a victory in the marathon category for privateers in the 1988 Paris-Dakar race. Although the following few years saw some more promising privateer results on the R100GS, the next chapter in the BMW Paris-Dakar saga belonged to the F650 single. In the meantime, BMW made the most of its four victories in this prestigious event, first offering Gaston Rahier replicas, then Paris-Dakar twins through until 1996.

The successful 1984 Paris-Dakar team of Hubert Auriol, Raymond Loizeaux, and the diminutive Gaston Rahier on the right. (BMW Mobile Tradition)

Rahier won the 1985 Paris-Dakar on this further developed desert racer, but was stricken with problems in the 1986 event. (BMW Mobile Tradition)

retained automotive style by three 12mm nuts. Similar to the ISDT machines were the 1.85 x 21in front and 2.15 x 18in rear wheels, and Metzeler developed tyres specifically suited to a large and powerful dual-purpose motorcycle. These were the first universal tyres to be rated at speeds up to 106mph (170kph). The front brake too was unusual for an enduro machine, with a single front disc and Brembo caliper, with the front master cylinder incorporated in the Magura throttle assembly. The rear brake was the usual rod-operated 200mm Simplex.

Also from the R65 came the angular fuel tank, but the plastic mudguards and sidecovers were specific for the R80 G/S. There was a bright red/orange, or blue, seat, and special footpegs, gearshift lever, and rear brake pedal. The non-adjustable footpegs were a folding motocross type with saw-toothed tips, and the gearshift lever pivoted backwards on the frame. Only a centrestand was fitted, although black engine protection bars with an integral sidestand were optional. The instrumentation was also relatively basic, with only a speedometer and warning lights, although a tachometer, and quartz clock were optional. Incorporated in the instrument nacelle was a small 140mm (5.5in) Bosch H4 headlight.

Despite being marketed as an enduro motorcycle, the R80 G/S quickly found favour as a competent all rounder. With less weight, superior ground clearance, and a more rigid chassis, it was widely accepted as the finest handling boxer yet. Off-road performance was compromised, but the R80 G/S provided exceptional street capability. Even with the universal Metzeler tyres, it was so good on the street that it outshone many supposedly more sporting models, and could embarrass a far more powerful motorcycle on a twisting mountain road.

As the R80 G/S could go just about anywhere, and its release coincided with victory in the Paris-Dakar rally, it was an immediate success. More than 6,000 were sold in the first year of production, and it went on to become one of the most popular models throughout the early 1980s. There were only a few changes for 1982. The electric start was now standard, and the rear wheel rim was increased to a 2.50 x 18in. For 1984, there was a new gas-charged

rear shock absorber with a remote reservoir, along with a new rear brake lever.

Essentially unchanged since 1981, for 1985 the R80 G/S incorporated the engine developments of the revised R80-series. Inside the new cylinder heads were revised bases and supports for the rocker shafts, and to eliminate excessive valve noise there were new rockers with axial bearings and plastic washers. Further noise reduction came through the installation of rubber buttons between the cylinder head fins. The valve seat material was also changed to overcome valve seat recession with unleaded fuel. During 1985 there was another new input shaft, kick-start spline, input helical driving gear, and thrust mount. The final drive assembly and casting for 1985 was also new, and included a new crown wheel set, and inner tapered roller bearing (from the K-series). There was also a larger 20Ah battery.

The R80 G/S continued virtually unchanged for 1986 and 1987 but for new colours and a differently shaped seat. There was a Paris-Dakar shielded muffler, and while the Paralever R80GS (without the '/' slash) replaced the R80 G/S for 1988, the earlier R80 G/S lived on as the R65GS, specifically for the German market. The 650cc (82 x 61.5mm) engine came from the R65, and with an 8.4:1 compression ratio and Bing 26mm carburettors produced 27bhp at 5,500rpm. The white R65GS looked visually identical to the 1987 R80 G/S but even in Germany proved unpopular.

The R80ST

Joining the R80 G/S for 1983 was a pure street version, the R80ST. Very similar to the R80 G/S, with the same engine and Monolever chassis, the R80ST also incorporated a number of R65 and R100 components. As an amalgam of elements taken from various models, it was a parts bin creation, and was seen as such. This was unfortunate, as the R80ST was even more competent on the street than the acclaimed R80 G/S, and must qualify as one of the most unappreciated of all BMW motorcycles. Some, like the R45 and R65, are justifiably forgotten, but the R80ST deserved better.

There were only detail differences in the engine between the R80ST and R80 G/S. The R80ST had the same deeper sump as R100 twins from 1981, with no protective sump plate, and there was no standard kick-start. The two-

into-one exhaust system was similar to that of
the R80 G/S, but chrome-plated, and
incorporated an insulated black cover plate. The
R80ST was also the first model to feature the
revised gearshift cam plate, but this soon carried
through to the entire range. As starting was
electric only, it included the larger 16Ah battery
of the electric start R80 G/S.

While the frame and Monolever swingarm
was shared with the R80 G/S, there was a
different front fork and rear shock absorber.
Some early brochures displayed the R80ST with
the R80 G/S leading axle front fork, but
production examples included an R65-style
centre axle fork. The fork legs provided for dual
front disc brakes, and the fork tubes were
longer than those of the R65. Compared to the
R80 G/S the fork travel was less, at 175mm
(6.9in), while the shortened R80 G/S Boge
shock absorber at the rear also provided less
travel (153mm/6.0in). Unique to the R80ST was
a wire-spoked 1.85 x 19in front wheel, while
the rear 2.50 x 18in was shared with the R80

Although derived from the successful R80 G/S, the street R80ST wasn't as successful. (Ian Falloon)

The R80ST featured traditional wire-spoked wheels, but the styling was uncohesive. (Cycle World)

Opposite: A Gaston Rahier signature on the fuel tank set the Paris-Dakar model apart from the standard R80 G/S. (Ian Falloon)

As a reliable adventure tourer the R80 G/S Paris-Dakar was unsurpassed. (Ian Falloon)

G/S. Also shared with the latter were the single Brembo front disc and 200mm rear Simplex drum brake.

Most of the bodywork was similar to that of the R80 G/S. The 19-litre (4.2gal) fuel tank was slightly smaller, and there was a low plastic front mudguard. Where the R80ST departed from the R80 G/S was in the inclusion of the R65 instrument panel with 100mm (3.9in) speedometer and tachometer, and central ignition and headlight switch. The 160mm (6.3in) Bosch H4 headlight was also from the R65. Standard on the R80ST were chrome-plated engine protection bars, with an integral sidestand with dual springs.

Although on paper the R80ST looked to have all the credentials for the perfect street motorcycle, it was not only viewed as a parts bin special, but was also considered an

anachronism. Wire-spoked wheels were unfashionable for street motorcycles in the early 1980s, as were 19in front wheels. The long front forks provided a stilted, elevated look, and the enduro-style high-rise exhaust system looked incongruous. On top of these impediments, performance was only moderate. Just 5,963 were produced, and the R80ST was a motorcycle for the connoisseur. Though it received favourable press coverage, it was the wrong motorcycle for the era.

The R80 G/S Paris-Dakar

Responding to its success in the Paris-Dakar rallies, a special Paris-Dakar version of the R80 G/S became available during 1984. While the engine and chassis were unchanged, setting the Paris-Dakar apart was a large, 32-litre (7gal) steel fuel tank, complete with Paris-Dakar rally winner Gaston Rahier's signature. There were red and blue Motorsport decals, foam kneepads, and enough fuel capacity to allow for 300 miles (480km) between stops. The fenders were white plastic, with a different rear fender, and there were no longer any plastic sidecovers. Also setting the Paris-Dakar apart was a red solo seat, with fixed black luggage rack. Access under the seat required removal of the rack, which was rather inconvenient. While the exhaust header pipes were still black, there was a stainless steel muffler with a black cover. The battery was a larger 20Ah, the black engine protection bars and sidestand were standard, and the weight went up to 205kg (451lb). All the Paris-Dakar equipment was available as a kit for the R80 G/S, and the Paris-Dakar edition was offered for 1985, 1986, and 1987.

Unlike the R45, R65, and R80ST, the success of the R80 G/S exceeded expectations. It was a brilliantly conceived motorcycle and its timing was perfect. Buoyed by success in the Paris-Dakar rally, production numbered 21,864 through until 1987. With the R80 G/S BMW found a unique formula, one that suited many adventure riders around the world, and particularly those in Germany and Italy. When the competition woke up to the R80 G/S's success it was already firmly entrenched. Although the replacement Paralever R100GS was also hugely popular, the lighter and smaller R80 G/S was the first of its kind. It is now considered the classic BMW *Gelände Strasse* motorcycle.

7 Refusing to die

From 1985 the R80RT featured a Monolever swingarm and new front end. US examples like this incorporated the SAS emission set-up.
(Cycle World)

With BMW's dubious commitment to the water-cooled, fuel-injected K-series, the future of the traditional twin looked uncertain. Although the engine was at the peak of its development, the Paris-Dakar victories and the subsequent success of the R80 G/S ensured that the boxer wouldn't die peacefully. The K100 replaced the R100 as expected, and the K75 was intended as BMW's middleweight, but the boxer remained in the post-1984 line-up. This was not only as

the G/S, but also in revamped 650 and 800cc guises. It seemed the new twins were only produced to maintain a classic tradition, and there was only minimal development. Soon, though, it was evident that the K-series wasn't the salvation BMW anticipated, and by 1988 a new range of 1,000cc air-cooled twins joined the 650 and 800cc versions. The resurrected R100RS and R100RT appealed to traditionalists, but the Paralever R100GS would

sustain the air-cooled boxer twin through until the advent of the next generation boxer, the R259.

The R80, R80RT, and R65

Although the K-series represented a radical departure from the traditional BMW motorcycle concept, the R80 and R65 harked back to the days when BMW and conservatism were analogous. Instead of more power, weight, and complexity, the new boxer twins reiterated the traditional BMW formula: simplicity, agility, and lightness were placed ahead of horsepower. Looking remarkably similar to the pre-1984 twins, the new R80 and R65 offered improved brakes and handling, but the performance was no match for the earlier R100. As with the R45, there was a special 27bhp R65 specifically for the German market.

The 800 and 650cc engines were essentially the same as the R80ST, but with some developments to reduce noise. Silicon-rubber plugs were fitted between the cooling fins, and there was a revised rocker arm assembly with

tight-fitting spacers between rocker arms and support brackets. There was little change to the general engine specifications from the R80ST. The valve sizes were 42 and 38mm (38 and 34mm on the R65), and electronic ignition was still Bosch TSZH. Carburation was by Bing V64 32mm carburettors, and there was a new, but restrictive, exhaust system. A large welded pre-muffler interconnected the left and right exhaust pipes before the twin mufflers, retaining the horsepower of the previous engine, but was a claimed three decibels quieter. From 1991, the US-style Secondary Air System was available as an option in all markets. Designed to reduce HC emissions by 30 per cent and CO emissions by 40 per cent, the SAS used exhaust pressure pulses to move two diaphragm valves in the air filter housing, drawing in fresh air. Two tubes directed this fresh air into the cylinder head and exhaust system behind the exhaust valve.

Considering the basic design was 15 years old, it was surprising to see continued modification to the gearbox to improve gear

The R80 from 1985 looked visually similar to earlier examples, but the chassis was updated. (Ian Falloon)

R80RT, R80, and R65
specifications (1985–95)

	R80RT	R80	R65
Bore (mm)	84.8	84.8	82
Stroke (mm)	70.6	70.6	61.5
Capacity (cc)	797	797	650
Compression ratio	8.2:1	8.2:1	8.7:1
Horsepower DIN	50@6,500 rpm	50@6,500 rpm	48@7,250 rpm
Left carburettor	Bing V64/32/305	Bing V64/32/305	Bing V64/32/359
Right carburettor	Bing V64/32/306	Bing V64/32/306	Bing V64/32/360
Overall width	960mm (37.8in)	800mm (31.5in)	800mm (31.5in)
Overall length	2,170mm (85.6in)	2,170mm (85.6in)	2,170mm (85.6in)
Wheelbase	1,447mm (57.0in)	1,447mm (57.0in)	1,447mm (57.0in)
Weight including oil but without fuel	207kg (455.4lb)	190kg (419lb)	183kg (402.6lb)
Weight including oil and fuel	227kg (499.4lb)	210kg (462lb)	205kg (451lb)
Top speed	170kph (106mph)	178kph (111mph)	174kph (108mph)

selection. During 1985 there was a new gearbox input shaft, and a new input helical driving layshaft with a 17.5° gear cut replacing the previous 15°. There was also a new gearlever bush and gear cam, with a further modification to the cam for 1987, when a new clutch pushrod and release bearing also appeared. The final drive assembly was now similar to the K-series, with a lighter and more substantial casting and stronger bearings.

Most of the updates for the new boxer were to the chassis, and comprised components from the R80ST and K-series. The frame was from the R80ST, with a twin loop main frame similar to that of the first /5, with a Monolever swingarm. The wheels, brakes, and suspension were similar to the K-series, with a K75-style centre-axle 38.5mm fork, providing considerably less travel than before (175mm/6.87in). It also incorporated an integral fork brace, a larger diameter (25mm) hollow axle, and provided for forward mounting of the Brembo brake calipers. From 1992 the front fork was a Marzocchi unit.

At the rear was a single gas-charged Boge shock absorber, providing 121mm (4.76in) of travel, and attaching to the trailing loop of the main frame via a forged steel mount. It also mounted on the rear axle housing (like the K-series) rather than the swingarm, the laid-down position resulting in a higher leverage ratio than on the R80 G/S and R80ST. The location of the single shock absorber also contributed to increased rigidity over the previous twin-shock type, and, combined with the sturdier front fork, the handling was more surefooted. There was certainly less of the *Gummi Kas* with the new chassis, although it was hardly state-of-the-art.

The front and rear cast alloy 2.50 x 18in wheels were also similar to those on the K-series, and not unlike the design for the R65LS except that they now accommodated tubeless tyres. The Y-fork and H-cross section was designed to provide spoke elasticity with rim rigidity. The rear wheel incorporated a 200mm drum brake, and the rear hub differed to the R80 G/S and R80ST in that it had four lug bolts rather than three. For 1990 there was an improved rear drum brake, with wider brake pads. A very narrow 90/90H18 front tyre contributed to agile steering without compromising braking performance, but high-speed stability wasn't as good as the previous model with the 19in front wheel. Somehow, the smaller front wheel also looked out of place, upsetting the balanced aesthetics of the earlier examples.

The front brake was upgraded to K-series specification, with a larger slotted 285mm disc with dual piston Brembo caliper. Some R80s had a dual disc fitted as standard, and the single disc from 1986 was the solid type of the R100GS. From 1991 on this became the drilled semi-floating type of the R100R, while twin disc examples still featured the slotted type.

Many classic features were retained for the R65 and R80. The fuel tank was the same shape as the previous R100, although the capacity was reduced to 22 litres (4.8gal) to accommodate some of the electrical components on the frame backbone tube. All the other bodywork was new, and arguably less attractive. Although the narrower seat continued the previous theme, the abbreviated plastic front fender was more angular, and there were new sidecovers that allowed visual checking of the battery. Continuing the classic theme were the earlier smaller diameter instruments, although the ignition key was moved to the handlebar

84

protective cover. There were also new handlebar switches, unlike, and more logical than, those of the contemporary K-series.

Alongside the R80 was a Monolever R80RT. The equipment was upgraded, the fairing now incorporating a clock and voltmeter, but the performance was similar to its predecessor. Somehow, despite its leisurely performance, the R80RT gained a following amongst touring riders who weren't in a hurry, but required agile handling, and it remained in production until 1995. With more than 22,000 produced, it was also the most popular of the post-1984 pure street air-cooled twins. Although not as popular (13,815 being produced), the R80 was also available until the end of 1995, but the similar R65 finished in 1993 with production ending at 8,260.

The introduction of the new R1100R boxer in 1994 signalled the demise of the naked R80. Apart from aesthetics and more weight, the R1100R was superior in nearly every respect. Although the R80 was produced to appeal to the traditionalist, functionally it offered little improvement over the pre-1984 examples and

was considered characterless. The performance was barely acceptable and it was outdated by the mid-1990s. On the other hand, the R1100R was a motorcycle that looked ahead, combining traditional and modern attributes.

R100RS, R100RT, and R100

As demand for the R80RT and R80 remained strong, and the K100 didn't receive unanimous support, there was a call for the return of the 1,000cc boxer. Late in 1986 the R100RS was re-released, initially as a run of just 1,000 examples, but response was so positive that the R100RS became a regular model for the 1988 model year, when it was also joined by a new R100RT. However, although interest in the R100RS was initially quite strong it gradually diminished, and by 1992 was virtually non-existent. It seemed that those who clamoured for the R100RS were dismayed when it appeared as a larger R80 and in a lower state of tune than the original R100RS. This was less of a concern with the R100RT, although this

Despite only providing moderate performance, demand for the older R100RT saw it continue through until 1996. (BMW Mobile Tradition)

R100RS and R100RT
specifications (1986–96)

	R100RS	R100RT
Bore (mm)	94	94
Stroke (mm)	70.6	70.6
Capacity (cc)	980	980
Compression ratio	8.45:1	8.45:1
Horsepower DIN	60@6,500rpm	60@6,500rpm
Left carburettor	Bing V64/32/363	Bing V64/32/363
Right carburettor	Bing V64/32/364	Bing V64/32/364
Overall width	800mm (31.5in)	960mm (37.79in)
Overall length	2,175mm (85.7in)	2,175mm (85.7in)
Wheelbase	1,447mm (57.0in)	1,447mm (57.0in)
Weight including oil but without fuel	210kg (461lb)	214kg (471lb)
Weight including oil and fuel	229kg (505lb)	234kg (515lb)
Top speed	187kph (116mph)	175kph (109mph)

model was not as popular as the smaller R80RT. The R100RT ran through until the end of 1995, but it was very much a niche market model by that stage. For 1991, the R100 also made a return, but only for the US market. Essentially an R80 with the R100RS/RT engine, it only lasted one year and was replaced by the R100R for 1992.

Increasing noise and emission controls (instigated in Europe from 1988) particularly hurt the large capacity air-cooled boxer, and the resurrected R100RS was no longer a high performance motorcycle. Derived from the R80, the 1,000cc engine was designed to provide more relaxed power over a wider rev range, and run on regular unleaded fuel. Compared to the earlier R100, the inlet valves were downsized to 42mm, there were 32mm Bing carburettors, and the quieter exhaust system with large pre-muffler was fitted. Both the R100RS and R100RT included a standard oil cooler, but in all other respects the engine was as for the R80. Although the engine was detuned, the emphasis on mid-range power actually provided improved on-the-road performance, although the new

The R100RS was resurrected in 1986 but didn't prove as popular as anticipated. One of the final versions was this Rennsport 30 of 1992. (Ian Falloon)

R100RS was down on top speed compared to earlier examples.

Both the R100RS and R100RT chassis were similar to the Monolever R80. The front fork was the same K-series type with 38.5mm fork tubes, and there was a single Boge rear shock absorber. Twin front disc brakes were standard, but cost cutting extended to the R80 rear drum rather than a disc, as on the pre-1985 RS and RT. With an 18in front wheel and shorter wheelbase, the new R100RS was more agile than its predecessor, and the Monolever chassis and stronger front fork provided improved handling.

One characteristic that wasn't changed was the superb R100RS fairing, still a benchmark in design a decade after it was released. The front section included the vented grille of the pre-1979 R100RS, along with an oil cooler at the top. The R100RT bodywork was identical to that of the R80RT, and no hydraulic steering damper featured on either model. Only a few R100RSs were built during 1990 and 1991, but as a final effort before the advent of the R1100RS nearly 1,000 were produced in 1992. Now with a Marzocchi front fork, there was

also a special series of 30 Rennsport models in traditional blue and silver, with a numbered plaque. The R100RT continued for a few more years with little change, ending with the Classic, offered for 1995 and into 1996.

R100GS, R100GS Paris-Dakar, and R80GS (1987–96)

While the resurrected R100RS failed to recreate its classic forebear, the rejuvenated R100 and R80GS expanded and improved the *Gelände Strasse* initiated by the classic R80 G/S. To imply a change in direction to off-road sports, the slash between the G and S disappeared, and the Monolever chassis was further developed to include a double universal joint and Paralever. The R80, R100RS, and R100RT didn't provide any technological improvement over earlier models, but the new GS was substantially developed and virtually all-new. Compared to the previous G/S, the GS was also a significantly larger motorcycle, with all the dimensions

The first Paralever BMW motorcycle was the R100GS. Though the colours were quite radical for 1988 the R100GS was extremely successful. (BMW Mobile Tradition)

R100GS, R100GS PD, and R80GS
specifications (1987–96)

	R100GS	R100GS PD	R80GS
Bore (mm)	94	94	84.8
Stroke (mm)	70.6	70.6	70.6
Capacity (cc)	980	980	798
Compression ratio	8.5:1	8.5:1	8.2:1
Horsepower DIN	60@6,500rpm	60@6,500rpm	50@6,500rpm
Left carburettor	Bing V64 II 94/40/123	Bing V64 II 94/40/123	Bing V64 II 64/32/349
Right carburettor	Bing V64 II 94/40/124	Bing V64 II 94/40/124	Bing V64 II 64/32/350
Overall width	830mm (32.7in)	830mm (32.7in)	830mm (32.7in)
Overall length	2,290mm (90.2in)	2,290mm (90.2in)	2,290mm (90.2in)
Wheelbase	1,514mm (59.6in)	1,514mm (59.6in)	1,514mm (59.6in)
Weight including oil but without fuel	197kg (433lb); 207kg (455lb) from 1991	197kg (433lb); 207kg (455lb) from 1991	187kg (411lb); 192kg (422lb) from 1991
Weight including oil and fuel	220kg (484lb); 236kg (519lb) from 1991	220kg (484lb); 236kg (519lb) from 1991	210kg (462lb); 215kg (473lb) from 1991
Top speed	180kph (112mph)	180kph (112mph)	168kph (104mph)

Although virtually identical to the R100GS, the (usually) more subdued Paralever R80GS wasn't as popular. (Ian Falloon)

increased. This didn't deter buyers, and, as with its predecessor, the new GS was an immediate success. During 1988 and 1989 it was the best-selling model of any motorcycle in Germany.

Essentially the R100GS engine was that of the R100RS and R100RT, although there were Bing 40mm carburettors. The R80GS engine also differed slightly to the R80 in that it had larger (40mm) exhaust valves, and both GSs featured a larger (3.8-litre) pre-silencer beneath the gearbox, improving the torque curve while reducing exhaust noise. New for the GS was a K-series type of layshaft electric start, including an intermediate planetary gear. The smaller electric motor saved 2kg (4lb), but the planetary gear provided the same torque. The R100GS also included a five-tier oil cooler, rubber-mounted on the right engine protection bar. When the R100GS was updated for 1991, there

were no engine developments apart from a larger sump.

Although the boxer engine was largely unchanged, the chassis was considerably updated, with the GS being the first BMW motorcycle to incorporate the Paralever swingarm. The frame was strengthened, with the oval tubes inside the backbone reinforced, although there was still no double tube as with the earlier twins. There was a stronger rear subframe and built-in luggage rack, along with a redesigned centrestand with more curved-out pedals. A sidestand was integrated with the left engine protection bar of the R100GS, but wasn't standard on the R80GS.

The real innovation was the Paralever swingarm, designed to minimise the effects of driveshaft movement under acceleration. The ideal swingarm length was an impractical 1,700mm (66.3in), so BMW's engineers René Hinsberg and Horst Brenner created the Paralever double-joint swingarm. Inside the single-sided swingarm was a second universal joint, freeing the rear gearcase and hub assembly and allowing it to float on the rear axle. An alloy strut connected the gearcase to the frame just below the swingarm pivot. Thus the swingarm, stay arm, gearcase, and frame formed a parallelogram, with pinion torque feeding into the lower strut instead of the swingarm. The slight fore and aft movement of the gearcase was absorbed by the laid down single shock absorber. As the parallelogram arrangement increased the radius of the wheel elevation curve, it provided the same effect as a 1,400mm (54.6in) swingarm.

Although the weight of the Paralever was 1.6kg (3.5lb) more, it allowed the increased travel (180mm/7.1in) of the Boge gas pressure shock absorber to be used more effectively. As with the R80, the shock absorber was bolted to the final drive housing, and for 1989 there was a softer shock absorber. An optional White Power sports suspension kit was also available for 1990, including replacement fork springs and a new rear shock absorber. Despite the advantages of the Paralever it still wasn't perfect, and the two needle roller bearings at the front coupling were especially prone to wear. They could even wear through the coupling yoke before the problem became apparent.

Complementing the Paralever swingarm were leading axle 40mm Marzocchi forks, with low

The 1990 R100GS Paris-Dakar provided improved off-road capability. (Ian Falloon)

friction Teflon coated sleeves, thicker aluminium triple clamps, fork brace, and a hollow 25mm axle. Spring travel was increased to 225mm (8.86in).

There were also innovative new wheels for the GS, the wire-spoke type allowing tubeless tyres. These cross-spoked wheels featured straight-pull spokes laced from the extreme edges of the rim, with the adjusting nipples in the hub. The crosswise arrangement of the spokes was claimed to increase torsional rigidity, and permitted replacement or adjustment of spokes without removal of the wheel. As with the R80, the rear wheel was retained by four lug nuts. The aluminium rims were 1.85 x 21in on the front and 2.50 x 17in on the rear. The front brake on the GS was a single undrilled 285mm disc, with a Brembo twin piston caliper, while the rear brake was a 200mm drum, now cable actuated. All these developments contributed to the GS being a more effective tarmac motorcycle than the R100RS and R100RT, being let down only by its lack of wind protection.

The 26-litre (5.7gal) fuel tank was new, and was 25mm (1.0in) shorter than on the R80 G/S. Although the GS was promoted as a dual-purpose machine, the emphasis was still on street use, and from 1989 there was an upper and lower mounting point for the front mudguard. Similar to the previous G/S was a sparse instrument layout, a single speedometer

being flanked by a series of warning lights. The R100GS included a taller nacelle above the 140mm (5.5in) headlight. For those riders who felt the R100GS too low, there was an even higher 880mm (34.6in) seat available.

Despite the fact that the last Paris-Dakar victory was beginning to fade into a distant memory, a Paris-Dakar kit was offered for the R80GS and R100GS during 1989. Then for 1990 BMW produced the R100GS Paris-Dakar, the largest and most expensive dirt bike available. Although its size was intimidating, the Paris-Dakar was an extremely successful niche model, mainly because nothing else like it was available. It also formed the basis of the next GS revision, for 1991.

Underneath the gargantuan R100GS Paris-Dakar was a standard R100GS, but the additional features were distinctive. Dominating the machine was a huge 35-litre (7.7gal) fuel tank with racing Paris-Dakar graphics, and a lockable 5-litre storage compartment. With the fuel tank came a frame and handlebar-mounted reinforced fibreglass fairing. The fairing side sections connected to the fuel tank, and like the racing Paris-Dakar bikes there was an external tubular fairing support. This incorporated a rectangular K75S headlight with a grilled protective rock guard. In addition to the standard GS instrument layout, the Paris-Dakar included a small tachometer and matching quartz clock.

After one year the R100GS Paris-Dakar was revised, with the emphasis featuring on-road rather than off-road proficiency. (Ian Falloon)

The final R100GS was the PD Classic of 1995 and 1996, with chrome-plated fairing supports and the older style rocker covers. (BMW Mobile Tradition)

Other components specific to the Paris-Dakar were a larger engine sump protector, also covering the frame and exhaust system, and plastic protective covers around the engine protection bars. A solo seat with longer luggage rack was standard, and a unique touch was the availability of the Paris-Dakar in plain primer paint, allowing the owner to customise the paintwork.

For 1991 the entire GS range was updated, not only incorporating many of the 1990 Paris-Dakar features but also emphasising road rather than off-road use. All models now included the cockpit fairing with external tubular frame and rectangular headlight, and an adjustable windshield that could tilt back and forth 75mm (3in). There was a new instrument layout, with a larger speedometer and tachometer, and the handlebar switches were from the K-series with separate switches either side for the turn signals. The indicators weren't self-cancelling because the GS speedometer wasn't electronic. Chassis improvements included an adjustable Bilstein rear shock absorber, providing ten positions for rebound damping, and a thinner (285 x 5mm) semi-floating front disc rotor. For the GS there was a smaller 24-litre (5.3gal) fuel tank, a low-mounted front mudguard, and a tougher seat.

With the release of the new R1100GS imminent, apart from some very garish graphics

The R1

While BMW struggled to find a performance identity with the K-series and resurrected boxer, during 1993 it investigated an alternative boxer twin, the R1. Compared with the current air-cooled design, the R1 was a true high performance engine. Liquid-cooled, with four valves per cylinder and twin chain-driven (four chains) overhead camshafts, the 98 x 66mm engine displaced 996cc. The exhaust camshaft was positioned lower in the cylinder head for improved ground clearance and to provide room for the

rider's feet, and the exhaust fed downwards, with the intakes directly above. The valve system was desmodromic, and the valves were set at an extremely shallow 20°. This allowed for a very flat piston, but there was still provision for three spark plugs per cylinder as on some of BMW's Formula 2 car racing engines two decades earlier. With Bosch electronic fuel injection, the power was around 140bhp and the engine was placed very high in the frame, with the alternator and starter underneath rather than on top. The airbox was concealed underneath the fuel tank.

The chassis was thoroughly up to date, with an aluminium twin-spar frame, wide

17in Marvic wheels, Brembo racing brakes, and the Telelever/Paralever front and rear suspension systems that were well developed by 1990. Because of the large aluminium longitudinal A-arm, there were twin side-mounted radiators, with cooling assisted by aircraft-style ducting. Although the most radical rendition yet of the boxer twin, BMW decided the R1 wasn't the design required to save the boxer. Water-cooling negated the benefits of two cylinders out in the airstream, and the limitations of engine width remained. The R1 didn't make it past the prototype stage, but it was undoubtedly the most effective sporting boxer twin ever created.

and colours there were no further changes to the R100GS and R80GS through until production ended. The final version was a Paris-Dakar 'farewell model', titled the R100GS PD Classic. Available in 1995 and into 1996, the fairing support and engine protection bars were chrome-plated and the handlebar levers silver epoxy-coated. There was a wider, high mounted front mudguard, the older R68-style round rocker covers, heated handlebar grips, and all models came with the SAS secondary air induction system. The R80GS continued for 1996 as the R80GS Basic, primarily for the German market. Essentially an earlier R80GS with a small fuel tank and headlight cowl, this also included the Paralever swingarm and the rounder rocker covers. An R80GS Basic was also the final air-cooled boxer produced, the

last leaving the Spandau production line on 19 December 1996.

As it provided exemplary road performance, acceptable off-road behaviour, and created a niche market, the GS was the most popular post-1984 air-cooled boxer twin. It continued where the previous G/S left off, and, with 45,364 produced, paved the way for the equally successful R1100GS and R1150GS. But even in the wake of this new, more powerful but even larger and heavier GS, the older R100GS remained a superb, competent, all-purpose motorcycle.

The R100R, R80R, and Mystic

While the world was still waiting for the new generation R259 during 1992, the release of which was more than a year away, the R100R Roadster was created to maintain interest in the boxer. Based on the R100GS, and designed as a classic looking 'grassroots' machine, the R100R was surprisingly successful. During 1992 it was BMW's best-selling motorcycle, with more than 8,000 sales, accounting for almost a quarter of production. It was particularly popular in Germany. However, while there was no denying the functional superiority of its chassis over earlier street boxers, the styling and execution of the R100R were questionable. Many cheap components detracted from what could have been one of BMW's classic motorcycles, and the R100R appeared to be another parts bin special like the R80ST.

R100R and R80R
specifications (1992–6)

	R100R	R80R (50bhp)
Overall width	719mm (28.3in)	719mm (28.3in)
Overall length	2,210mm (87.1in)	2,210mm (87.1in)
Wheelbase	1,495mm (58.8in)	1,495mm (58.8in)
Weight including oil but without fuel	197kg (433lb)	196kg (431lb)
Weight including oil and fuel	218kg (480lb)	217kg (478lb)
Top speed	181kph (112mph)	168kph (104mph)

As with the earlier R80ST, the R100R was based on its dual-purpose stable-mate, in this case the R100GS. Except for the different exhaust system and the older-style rocker covers, the R100R and R100GS engines were identical. Included on the R100R was the larger sump of the 1991 GS, lighter layshaft starter, and 40mm Bing carburettors (although US models retained 32mm carburettors). The exhaust system featured a large pre-muffler and low mounted stainless steel K100 muffler, and rather than mount the oil cooler on the engine protection bar like the GS, this was now positioned in front of the engine. The classic look even extended to the older-style spark plug caps, but the engine was still very similar to the 1981 version.

The frame and Paralever swingarm also came from the R100GS. The R100R was the first street boxer twin to include the Paralever, and it contributed to outstanding handling. For the first time on a BMW motorcycle, Japanese Showa suspension was used front and rear, the shorter non-adjustable 41mm front fork providing 135mm (5.3in) of travel. At the rear was a single Showa shock absorber, providing 140mm (5.5in) travel, with adjustable rebound

damping. This suspension was adequate but not exceptional.

Further emphasising the classic image were cross-spoked wheels, with Akront aluminium rims, a 2.50 x 18in on the front and 2.50 x 17in on the rear. The front brake was a single perforated floating 285 x 5mm disc, with a four-piston Brembo caliper from the K-series, while the cable-operated rear drum was the same as the GS. Also from the GS was the tall 24-litre (5.3gal) fuel tank, looking ungainly on the R100R. The round 180mm (7.1in) headlight came from the K75, while a cheap looking plastic nacelle contained the R100GS instruments. The foot controls were also similar to the GS, with the same reversed gearshift linkage. Styling considerations extended to the two-tone seat, with a silver rear rack, and if that looked too subdued there was an optional chrome kit. This comprised a chrome-plated fork stabiliser, valve covers, carburettor tops, instrument panel, direction indicator housings, fuel tank cap, mirrors, and exhaust nuts. Despite many dubious styling details, unlike the earlier R80ST the R100R was the right machine at the right time. Naked machines were beginning to reassert themselves, and although

The R100R was based on the R100GS, and proved to be a very successful adaptation. This is the final version, the Classic.
(BMW Mobile Tradition)

not powerful the R100R was light and the Paralever swingarm and shorter travel suspension contributed to arguably the finest handling boxer yet.

Joining the R100R for 1993 was a similar R80R, primarily for the German market, in 27bhp and 34bhp versions, but this was discontinued the following year. As 1993 was the year for the release of the R259, only cosmetic differences distinguished the 1993 R100R from the 1992 model. There were large, and particularly conspicuous, 'BOXER' emblems on the sides of the tank, and lurid turquoise green metallic paintwork. For 1994 the R100R received dual disc front brakes, the SAS emission system as standard, and there was a special Mystic version. The Mystic was a more successful adaptation of the classic concept, with many of the questionable features of the R100R replaced. Along with the red metallic paint there were number of chrome-plated items, including headlight support, instrument surround with new warning light set-up, and indicator supports. The Mystic also had a lower handlebar, restyled seat and tailpiece, new sidecovers, and a shorter licence plate support. As a result, the styling of the Mystic was more successful than the basic R100R, although functionally it was similar.

The R100R and Mystic continued for 1995

and into 1996, the R100R in a final 'farewell model' classic edition. The R100R Classic was black, with many components also highlighted in black, but otherwise was unchanged. Along with the R100 PD Classic, and the R100RT Classic, the R100R Classic and Mystic represented the end of the era instigated back in 1969 with von der Marwitz's /5. The most surprising thing about these final Classic editions was their similarity to the original design. There were some significant chassis developments along the way, but the basic engine and transmission were remarkably similar. Yet, just as the /2-series found itself out of touch at the end of the 1960s, so it was with the air-cooled boxer in the 1990s. Increasing noise and emission controls saw the air-cooled boxer struggling to maintain a respectable power output, and it had reached the limit of its development. The engine had served BMW well for more than 25 years but its time had come. Fortunately, the boxer wasn't about to die, and as interest in the K-series waned, BMW decided the future lay in a new generation boxer. This new design, the R259, built on the success of the air-cooled boxer, and continued the boxer tradition. In the process, the R259 introduced many more riders to the world of BMW motorcycles, and would go on to become the most successful boxer twin of all.

The final four air-cooled boxers were the Classic models of 1995 and 1996. (BMW Mobile Tradition)

Opposite: A variation on the R100R was the Mystic, with more chrome and special metallic paint. (BMW Mobile Tradition)

95

8 New generation RS and RT

As soon as the K-series was released in 1984, work was instigated on a replacement for the R80 boxer. Unable to meet increasing noise and emission controls, it was inevitable that the life of the air-cooled design was limited, so a 'Boxer Workshop' was created. This was initially under the guidance of Stefan Pachernegg, co-ordinator of the K-series project. At that time it was

envisaged that the K-series would rescue motorcycle sales, and the new boxer was to be a mid-range, 800cc supplement to the K-series.

Even in the early stages, the design parameters were clear. The traditional longitudinal boxer twin with protruding cylinders would be maintained, with the exhaust at the front and the intake at the rear.

96

Tradition dictated air-cooling, and the load-bearing crankcase would contribute to the frame structure. To maintain the superior torque-curve of the two-cylinder engine, but with increased power, four valves per cylinder were considered a necessity. Most discussion centred on the design of a suitable valve train. While the existing overhead valve design, with a single camshaft, long pushrods, and rockers in the cylinder head, was noisy and lacked stiffness, a conventional double overhead camshaft layout was ruled out because of increased engine width. Other designs evaluated included a bevel gear driven shaft operating the valves through short tappets and rockers, and a reciprocating oscillating rod drive to two overhead camshafts. It wasn't until 1986, when Georg Emmersberger proposed a hybrid system, that a suitable solution was found.

Before this, work was already progressing on the design of a self-supporting engine block, and the development of a new front suspension system. While often considered a conservative company, innovative frame and suspension design has typified BMW motorcycles throughout their history. From the R32, with one of the first closed-loop tubular steel frames, to the R12 and R17 of 1935 with telescopic forks, and the Earles fork twins of 1955, BMW had dared to tread a different path. So it was with the new R259 boxer. Although other manufacturers maintained their allegiance to the conventional telescopic front fork, BMW's engineers were determined to overcome some of the inherent deficiencies in this design. These included excessive brake dive, changes in camber under movement, and a whiplash effect. The earlier Earles fork solved some of these problems, but at the expense of substantial unsprung weight and extreme steering inertia. The new solution combined a telescopic fork with support arms on the frame, first patented by Laurence W. King and John K. Pizzey in Britain in the early 1970s. Their system linked the lower end of the telescopic fork with support arms, but did not really overcome the problem of unsprung weight.

In 1981, British engineer Hugh Nicol submitted details of his Nicol Link Suspension System to the BMW Motorcycle Development Department. Combining the telescopic fork with a longitudinal arm linking the fork bridge to the frame, this design was the breakthrough BMW was looking for. Coincidentally, Phil Todd and Nigel Hill produced the Motodd Laverda at around the same time, with an identical suspension layout to Nicols's. Nicols sent a copy of a favourable journalist's test report of the Motodd machine to BMW, who reconsidered his design. They soon concluded it to be the ideal solution for front wheel suspension and wheel guidance. Günter Baron in the Prototype Testing Department had already built a problematic K100 test machine, and this was modified with new bearing positions. But it was the new boxer engine, without the limitations of a radiator position and with a self-supporting engine block, which provided the best solution for a new front wheel suspension set-up.

A longitudinal track control arm transmitted braking forces directly into the rigid engine block, effectively providing anti-dive, with a ball bearing connecting the telescopic fork with the A-shaped control arm. A second ball bearing connected the upper fork bridge with a central mounting point on the frame. The telescopic fork only served the purpose of guiding and steering the front wheel, with a single centrally-mounted spring strut attached to the longitudinal arm responsible for suspension and damping. The result was improved stability, with minimal additional unsprung weight and changes to camber.

By 1985 substantial progress had already been made on the development of the front suspension, and various solutions were

The rear view of the new boxer engine, demonstrating Emmersberger's valve drive solution. (BMW Mobile Tradition)

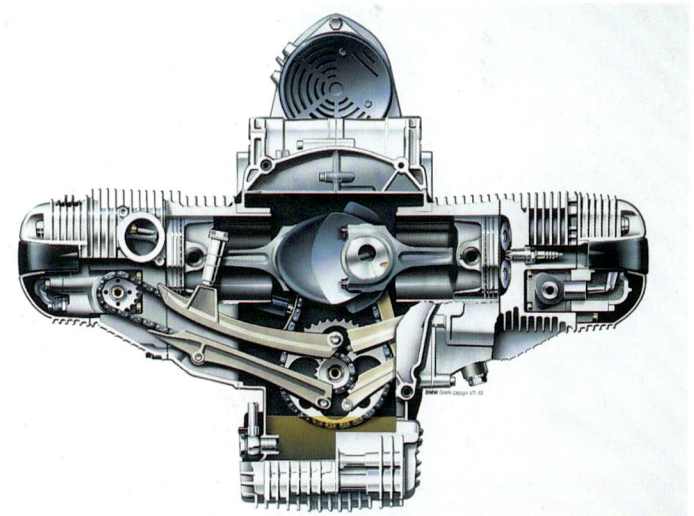

*By 1988 the R259
bodywork wasn't
finalised, and the engine
included Bing
carburettors. The rear
shock absorber was still
positioned on the side of
the swingarm. (BMW
Mobile Tradition)*

investigated to find a suitable valve drive system
for the new boxer. Drive by a vertical shaft and
bevel gears was excessively noisy and expensive
to manufacture, and Emmersberger's design was
chosen, as it was relatively simple and saved
40mm (1.6in) of engine width compared to a
conventional double overhead camshaft design.
The valve system featured an intermediate shaft
beneath the crankshaft, with two roller chains
driving a single camshaft in each cylinder head.
The camshafts were below the four valves, and
actuated by rockers through short pushrods
with ball heads. The project was given the
designation R259, and the project manager was
Richard Kramhöller. The resultant engine was
known as the A60 and A61.

Development proceeded, with the first
prototype running by April 1987. By this stage
demand for the R-series boxer had increased
significantly, and market considerations
required the new boxer to effectively compete
with four-cylinder touring motorcycles. The
engine was now to be 1,000cc, but there were
still problems with the valve train mechanism.
The first of seven prototype engines produced
84bhp in February 1988, but the pushrods
floated above 7,000rpm. The next step saw the
camshafts and rocker arm supports mounted in
a separate sub-assembly rather than the
camshafts being mounted directly in the cylinder
head. Seizure of the rocker arms caused by the
cup-shaped tappets led to open tappets with
short pushrods. As these proved too heavy, the
eventual solution was found with chill-cast
bucket followers with steel ball heads on either
end of the short aluminium pushrods. After
completion of the prototype in May 1988, the
R259 was presented to the management in
October. The project received the go-ahead for
further technical development, but not for the
styling, as it was deemed appropriate to involve
the car stylists from BMW AG and BMW
Technik.

During 1989 a prototype successfully
completed endurance tests over 10,000km
(6,100 miles), and the engine with the modified
valve train ran on the dyno for the first time.
These early prototypes had the alternator
mounted on the crankshaft, running in an oil
bath. Subsequent versions, with a more
sophisticated electronic control system, saw the
alternator moved on top of the engine and
driven by a poly-V-belt.

The first series R1100RS, with optional luggage. (BMW Mobile Tradition)

Engine development also wasn't trouble free, and throughout 1990 dyno and endurance testing revealed problems with vibration, noise, and cracked engine blocks. In preparation for production, the engine structure was reinforced, and the new head of development, Dr Burkhard Göschel, decided to increase capacity to 1,100cc. The earlier carburettors were discarded, and the previously optional Motronic fuel injection became standard.

During the second half of 1990 three motorcycles were undergoing major endurance testing, each machine covering 30,000km (19,000 miles) on Autobahns, country roads, and alpine passes. This testing showed the deficiencies in the front suspension, even with Teflon-coated bushes, that saw the installation of much longer sliding tubes (620 instead of 530mm), which were also smaller in diameter (35 instead of 40mm). The cast aluminium longitudinal control arm was also deemed too stiff as it transmitted excessive force into the engine mounts, and altering the length of the supporting tubular steel bars found the ideal geometry and wheelbase. The position of the shock absorber was also critical, and brake dive compensation was limited to 70 per cent. With

the final development of the front wheel control system in 1992 it became known as the BMW Telelever. The Paralever rear suspension was also modified at this time, with the single shock absorber positioned longitudinally in the middle of the wider cast-aluminium swingarm. This was initially square in section, but was later replaced by lighter and stronger round tubing.

Early in 1991 three 1,100cc fuel injected prototypes were subjected to exhaustive 30,000km tests. This time the valve control system and modified crankshaft presented no problems. The engine was comfortably producing 90bhp, and a larger 1.5-litre airbox contributed to a reduction in noise level to 79db(A). Further testing on the Nürburgring circuit finalised the suspension tuning, with the final endurance testing conducted with production components over 50,000km (30,000 miles) in the spring of 1992. By September that year the R259 was ready for unveiling at the Cologne Show.

The R1100RS

The engine designation was initially A60 (1,000cc) and later A61 (1,100cc). The crankcase was no longer the one-piece tunnel type, but a pressure die-cast, vertically-split, two-piece set-up that was more economical to manufacture. The two halves were bolted together, and included a 4.5-litre integral sump. As it was a load-bearing chassis component, the crankcase was strong and incorporated judicious reinforcing. Central to the design were four-valve cylinder heads, with two 36mm intake and two 31mm exhaust valves, and a central spark plug with three ground electrodes. The 'high cam' set-up had the camshafts mounted alongside the valves and not above them, driven by long roller chains from an intermediate shaft below the crankshaft. Instead of being one-piece the camshafts were comprised of several elements, with the sintered cams pressed on to a nitrided-steel shaft. The valve lift was 9.85mm on the inlet and 9.4mm on the exhaust, with a duration of 300°. The intake manifold was 50mm, and to improve gas flow the rear of the cylinder head was rotated 12° upwards.

Many of the other engine features were similar to earlier boxers, with nickel-silicon coated aluminium cylinders and a one-piece forged crankshaft with two main bearings. The con-rods featured crack technology, where the big-end was intentionally fractured to provide a larger surface area and perfect fit. It also eliminated the need for labour-intensive dowels.

The engine also included two separate oil circulation systems, one for lubrication, the other for cooling. Two Eaton pumps were housed in a separate unit on the front of the intermediate shaft, the cooling pump at the front and the lubrication pump at the rear. The cooling oil pump was designed to circulate as much oil as possible, with oil travelling to the cylinder heads and around the exhaust valves from the oil cooler to the sump. This lowered the temperature of the exhaust valve seats by 70°C.

Bosch Motronic MA 2.2 fuel injection with 50mm throttle intakes was installed on the new boxer. The air intake system was also updated, with air drawn through a snorkel beneath the fuel tank into the large airbox. A number of other features set the new engine apart from its predecessor. An electric fuel pump provided pressurised fuel to the injectors, and the CPU controlled the ignition as well as the fuel delivery. Sensors for throttle position, air and oil temperature, revs, and barometric pressure supplied information to the CPU. A catalytic converter was also available, incorporating an oxygen sensor. To power the electrical system was a three-phase 700-watt alternator and a smaller and lighter 19Ah battery. The Motronic system was well proven, but was a new step for the boxer. Boxers had traditionally appealed to those riders who wanted a simple motorcycle without daunting technology. The R259 changed all that, but it was soon evident that buyers were prepared to accept modern technology if it was functionally superior.

One area that wasn't new was the K-series derived 180mm single plate dry clutch, with the usual diaphragm spring, and three-shaft five-speed gearbox. Although the transmission driveshaft included an integral torsional spring vibration damper to smooth the power pulses, the gearbox remained the weakest component in the drivetrain.

With the decision made to pursue the use of Telelever front suspension, and to incorporate the engine as a load-bearing frame component, by the time the R1100RS entered production this chassis was well developed. The engine provided the support for both front and rear suspension, with an aluminium casting, braced by a pair of rearward extending steel tubes, forming the steering head. Front springing and damping was by a central non-adjustable Showa shock absorber, providing 120mm (4.73in) of front wheel travel. The Telelever not only allowed for excellent weight distribution – 52.7/47.3 per cent front and rear – but it improved stability, because the wheelbase and trail increased slightly under compression and reduced under rebound. The steering head angle was a reasonably steep 24.1°, with only 104mm (4.1in) of trail, but the most disconcerting aspect was handlebar movement, as this was attached to the upper moveable bridge and was rubber mounted. The rear shock absorber was also a Showa, with 135mm (5.32in) of travel.

The aluminium three-spoke wheels and brakes were identical to those of the K1 and K1100RS (3.50 x 17in on the front and 4.50 x 18in on the rear). The brakes were twin 305mm floating cross-drilled discs on the front with four-piston (32 and 34mm) Brembo calipers, and a single 285 x 5mm disc with a dual 38mm piston Brembo caliper on the rear. The R1100RS was also the first model to offer the second generation ABS II as an option.

101

R1100RS and R1100RT specifications

	R1100RS	R1100RT
Years	1993–2001	1996–2001
Bore (mm)	99	99
Stroke (mm)	70.5	70.5
Capacity (cc)	1,085	1,085
Compression ratio	10.7:1	10.7:1
Horsepower DIN	90@7,200rpm	90@7,200rpm
Overall width	920mm (36.2in)	898mm (35.4in)
Overall length	2,175mm (85.7in)	2,195mm (86.5in)
Wheelbase	1,467mm (57.8in)	1,485mm (58.5in)
Weight including oil and fuel	239kg (527lb)	282kg (622lb)
Top speed	215kph (133mph)	196kph (122mph)

The R1100RS was also available with a full fairing. (BMW Mobile Tradition)

Initially the R259 was a continuation of the sport-touring RS theme initiated with the R100RS back in 1977 and continued with the K100RS in 1984. However, the styling for the R259 proved more difficult than expected, and despite the creation of four full-size scale models it wasn't until April 1990 that the styling layout was approved. Early prototypes used a K100RS-style fairing and testing was completed in BMW's wind tunnel in South Africa. Eventually a solution was found that merged the plastic 23-litre (5gal) fuel tank with the fairing to envelope the sides of the motorcycle. One of the designers' tasks was to provide an ergonomic design for the windshield, controls, and seat, with individual adjustment allowing maximum flexibility. They managed to provide a fuel tank around the large alternator on top of the engine and the front subframe. Despite this intensive design work, however, the R1100RS wasn't one of BMW's most successful styling efforts, although the full fairing option was an improvement.

It may not have been particularly light, or classically beautiful, but the R1100RS was undoubtedly the most functionally superior sport-touring motorcycle available. It also magnificently upheld the BMW RS tradition, and proved a worthy successor to the earlier R100RS. Although the A61 engine wasn't

hugely powerful, the significantly higher torque in the mid and higher rpm range ensured vastly improved on-the-road performance over the older A10 engine that powered the R100 and R80.

Over the next few years the R1100RS underwent only minimal development. Tighter tolerances and O-rings cured gearbox complaints, and the front Showa shock absorber was upgraded to include adjustable rebound damping. The ergonomic kit (including adjustable seat height and handlebar) became standard, as did a catalytic converter. Although the final R1100RS of 2001 received larger (320mm) front brake discs and new generation EVO brake calipers, there were remarkably few changes to the basic design for nearly a decade, and 26,037 were produced. In the meantime, the R1100RS was overtaken in popularity by the R1100GS and to a lesser extent by the R1100R. In the wake of this success, a fourth new generation boxer, the R1100RT, appeared at the Frankfurt Motor Show in September 1995.

The R1100RT

By 1995 the RT concept was already well established as one of BMW's most successful. The R100RT of 1978 was the first production touring motorcycle with a wind tunnel-developed aerodynamic fairing, and subsequently the RT remained in continuous production through until 1996. Yet, while the fairing was aerodynamically efficient, and provided supreme rider protection, the twin-cylinder RT was always underpowered. This was especially noticeable with the R80RT and post-1987 R100RTs, and by 1995 the RT was crying out for a more powerful engine. Of course, there was always the option of the K1100LT, but this gargantuan four-cylinder tourer wasn't for the boxer enthusiast.

Unlike the earlier RTs that were identical to the parent RS underneath the bodywork, BMW gave the R1100RT an individual identity. While the engine and drivetrain were identical to the R1100RS (except for a lower 1:2.81 final drive ratio), the chassis was unique, and arguably superior to that of the RS. The front subframe came from the dual-purpose R1100GS, while the front shock absorber was shared with the R1100R. The Telelever A-arm came from the R1100RS, as did the rear subframe, pillion

footrest supports, and shock absorber. Spring preload for the rear shock was hydraulically adjustable, but the most noticeable advantage of the R1100RT over the R1100RS was the separately mounted handlebar of the R1100GS. Because the large handlebar would have amplified the motions of the Telelever, on the R1100RT the fork bridge and handlebar were connected to the Telelever tubes through two ball joints in the fork bridge. The handlebars were thus isolated from the Telelever tilt and swivel. As the R1100RT used a combination of suspension components the steering geometry was unique, with a steering head angle of 27.2° and 122mm (4.8in) of trail. Although the wheels and front brakes were from the R1100RS, second generation ABS was standard on the R1100RT. The rear brake included the smaller 276mm disc of the R1100GS.

Continuing the tradition of the much-loved R100RT, the R1100RT was extremely competent, and won the hearts of the touring fraternity. (Australian Motorcycle News)

The fairing and bodywork were developed specifically for the R1100RT, and were American designer David Robb's first boxer project. Robb created a large thermoplastic PRT and PC rubber fairing with a drag coefficient of 0.494 CdA. Incorporated in the fairing was a large windshield, electrically adjustable for rake by 22° and height by 155mm (6.1in). The mirrors were integrated into the fairing, and a two-piece front wheel cover connected to the lower fork bridge to minimise front wheel lift. At 26 litres (5.7gal) the fuel tank was larger than on the R1100RS, and the adjustable seat subdivided in two sections. Along with the small rectangular headlight, the side flush-fitting aluminium footpeg supporting panels lent an individual look to the R1100RT. In keeping with the touring nature, a wide range of options was available in addition to the standard 33-litre panniers. These included a cassette radio, heated handlebar grips, and a 30-litre top-box. For 1998 there was a special 75th Anniversary edition, but otherwise the R1100RT changed little during its lifespan.

Although still a large and heavy touring motorcycle, the R1100RT was the right machine at the right time. Whereas the four-cylinder K1100LT was moderately successful, with the R1100RT BMW had an immediate winner. It wasn't that it was especially functionally superior to the LT, but it was more modern, and as it was powered by the boxer engine it appealed to traditionalists. Production up until 2001 amounted to just over 53,000, making the R1100RT the world leader in touring motorcycles.

The R1150RT

In the spring of 2001 the R1100RT received the upgraded 1,130cc engine and six-speed gearbox that had appeared on the R1150GS in 2000 and on the R1150R a few months earlier. This engine was accompanied by some significant chassis and styling updates. While there were few complaints about the earlier 1,100cc boxer engine and the way it performed, the increase in torque (to 100Nm at 5,500rpm) made the R1150RT even more efficient as a touring motorcycle. And with more than 90Nm of torque between 3,000 and 6,500rpm the power was always available when required. This power was transmitted through a new, smaller (165mm) hydraulically operated clutch and the

The all-enveloping R1100RT fairing cocooned the rider and ensured a supremely comfortable touring environment. (Australian Motorcycle News)

Although it looked similar, a number of styling and technical updates distinguished the R1150RT from the R1100RT. (Australian Motorcycle News)

new six-speed gearbox. The sixth gear was effectively an overdrive. The engine management system was upgraded at the same time, to the digital Bosch MA 2.4 system first introduced on the R1100S in 1998. From 2003 the R1150RT (along with most other R259 boxers) received the new Getrag-built six-speed gearbox, with high-rise teeth and a larger overlap of the gear flanks to reduce noise. At the same time the gearbox dogs were modified to improve shifting.

Although the chassis and suspension were much as on the R1100RT, as the six-speed gearbox required a larger housing the swingarm was reduced in length from 520mm (20.5in) to 506mm (19.9in). The supports for the shock absorber, rear frame, and footpegs, were also modified. While the front wheel trail was unchanged, the fork angle was slightly less, at 27.1°. The new wheels were the most obvious improvement; the R1150RT adopting the beautiful finely-cast double five-spoke aluminium wheels of the R1100S. The front wheel was 460g lighter, and the rear saved 340g. While the reduction in unsprung weight had a positive practical benefit, so did the different rear wheel size of 5.00 x 17in. This allowed for a wider 170/60ZR17 tyre.

Also upgraded was the front braking system, now incorporating the EVO brake with 320mm discs and the new Integral ABS system. On the R1150RT this was the fully integrated version, with the hand and foot brakes acting simultaneously on the front and rear. After the

R1150RS and R1150RT *specifications*

	R1150RS	R1150RT
Years	2002–	2001–
Bore (mm)	101	101
Stroke (mm)	70.5	70.5
Capacity (cc)	1,130	1,130
Compression ratio	11.3:1	11.3:1
Horsepower DIN	95@7,250rpm	95@7,250rpm
Overall width	920mm (36.2in)	898mm (35.4in)
Overall length	2,170mm (85.6in)	2,230mm (87.8in)
Wheelbase	1,469mm (57.9in)	1,485mm (58.5in)
Weight including oil and fuel	248kg (547lb)	279kg (615lb)
Top speed	215kph (133mph)	200kph (124mph)

rather plump looking R1100RT the R1150RT also received a facelift, with more attractive tandem headlights, integrated with two fog lamps. The headlight was adjustable for height by a hand wheel, and a new front wheel cover accompanied the redesigned upper fairing. The plastic fuel tank had a capacity of 25.2 litres (5.5gal), and the filler now incorporated a rollover valve. And as if the R1100RT seat wasn't comfortable enough, the new seat incorporated more padding, although its height went up by 25mm (1.0in). In all other respects the R1150RT maintained the same high level of touring equipment as the R1100RT.

The R1150RS

By 2002 the original new boxer, R1100RS, was almost the forgotten model in the line-up. Although the senior machine, it was the firstborn and the least loved. To the surprise of many the new R1150RS maintained a similar face, presenting an almost old-fashioned image.

Compared to other updated new generation boxers, the R1150RS was an evolutionary development of the earlier version. (BMW)

Despite this, the RS still epitomised the finest attributes of sport-touring BMW motorcycles, falling comfortably between the extremes of sport and touring exemplified by the R1100S and R1150RT.

Although its engine and transmission were shared with the R1150RT, the R1150RS retained the basic chassis set-up of the R1100RS. Apart from the use of R1150RT fork tubes the front Telelever was from the R1100RS, although the shorter swingarm and rear shock absorber were from the R1150RT. The footpegs came from the R1150R, and the wheels were the same as on the more recent boxers. As expected, there was the EVO brake on the front wheel (claimed to improve braking power by 20 per cent), but the Integral ABS was only an option. On the R1150RS this was the partial system, with the hand operating both wheels and the foot pedal the rear only.

While the shape of the fairing was similar to the R1100RS, the adjustable windshield was 80mm (3.1in) higher and 60mm (2.4in) wider, significantly improving rider protection. The fairing enclosed the engine housing, like the previously optional full fairing, and there were new switches and controls. While there was now a 17in rear wheel, the R1150RS retained the larger 285mm rear disc brake. Certainly the R1150RS was a less comprehensive update to an existing design than the earlier 1150s, GS, R, and RT, and this prompted speculation as to whether it was a stopgap model in preparation for a completely new generation boxer.

Only new colours distinguished the 2003 R1150RS from the 2002 model. (BMW)

⑨ Gelände Strasse take three

Introduced for the 2000 model year, the R1150GS could be outfitted with full touring equipment. (Australian Motorcycle News)

Just as Richard Wagner changed the direction of German music in 1853 with his famous unresolved chord in the opera *Tristan and Isolde*, so did BMW alter the course of the German motorcycle with the R80 G/S. At a time when motorcycle sales were stagnating, the G/S steered BMW through a new, oblique path, creating its own successful niche market. And with the resurrection of the 1,000cc air-cooled boxer, the GS led the way. By 1993 *Gelände Strasse* was intrinsic to BMW vocabulary, and the R1100GS appeared only a year after the release of the R1100RS, being launched (as a 1994 model) at the Frankfurt Motor Show in September 1993. And, in the manner of previous GSs, it proved exceptionally successful, immediately becoming the most popular large displacement enduro in Germany.

The R1100GS and R850GS

With the R80 G/S BMW had initiated a tradition of features unique to the G/S series, and the R1100GS continued this. While the A61 engine came from the parent R1100RS, it was modified to provide improved enduro performance. With a lower compression ratio, milder camshafts, and a recalibrated Motronic fuel injection system, top end power was sacrificed to emphasise the mid-range. The peak power went down, the torque increased slightly (to 97Nm at 5,250rpm), and there was a lower final drive ratio.

Similar to the R1100RS was the three-piece frame, with the engine and transmission forming a single load-bearing unit, and the Telelever front suspension with single shock absorber. Revisions to the Telelever to make it more suitable for off-road use saw shock absorber travel increased to 190mm (7.48in), with the wide handlebar mounted on the fork bridge and connected to the Telelever fixed tubes with two ball joints in the fork bridge. This effectively isolated the handlebar from the tilt and swivel motions of the Telelever, contributing to a more conventional steering feel. What was unconventional, though, was the Telelever's resistance to dive under braking, and the modified A-arm and front subframe provided an increased anti-dive ratio of 90 per cent. The steering head angle was also a steeper 26°, with increased trail of 115mm. Updates to the rear shock absorber included a hydraulic spring preload adjuster, with travel increasing to 200mm (7.88in). Like the R100GS, the wheels were BMW's patented cross-spoke type, in sizes

The styling of the R1100GS was individual, and did little to disguise its size. (Australian Motorcycle News)

of 2.50 x 19in on the front and 4.00 x 17in on the rear. While the front braking system was shared with the R1100RS, the rear disc was smaller at 276mm. ABS II was available as an option, and could be manually deactivated so that the rider could lock the wheels in loose gravel if required.

A large, 25-litre (5.5gal) plastic fuel tank ensured an adequate touring range, and the R1100GS was equipped with a small cockpit fairing and windscreen, adjustable over a range of 13°. With four mudguards, including a beak-like guard to dust air to the oil cooler, the R1100GS imparted an unusual presence. Certainly not beautiful, for an off-road motorcycle it was also extremely large and heavy. The seat height of either 860mm (33.9in) or 840mm (33.1in) also guaranteed this was a motorcycle more suited to larger riders.

Beauty is always in the eye of the beholder, however, and the R1100GS met with astounding acclaim regardless of these impediments, and, in the manner of earlier GSs,

soon proved to be one of BMW's most capable tarmac burners. The combination of wide handlebar, unlimited ground clearance, and supple suspension meant that a well-ridden R1100GS could see off many pure sportsbikes, and it could be ridden off-road if required. For 1995 the lower front mudguard was moved forward 192mm (7.6in), and a three-way catalytic converter was standard from 1996. There was a special 75th Anniversary version for 1998, and for 1999 a similar R850GS. But somehow the concept of a smaller engine in this large motorcycle wasn't so appealing, and, apart from specific low output versions to meet European regulations, the R850GS wasn't as popular.

Despite selling more than 45,000, the R1100GS (and R850GS) wasn't perfect or trouble free. Problems with the chassis cracking at the gearbox frame mount led to several interim modifications, and it was no surprise that the first of the new 1150 series was the R1150GS. The R850GS continued as before for

Opposite: One advantage of the R1100GS over earlier examples was the increased power, more than enough to lift the front wheel. (Australian Motorcycle News)

For 1996 the R1100GS styling was less radical, but it was still an unusual looking motorcycle. (BMW)

R1100GS R850GS, R1150GS, and R1150GS Adventure specifications

	R1100GS	R850GS	R1150GS	R1150GS Adventure
Years	1994–9	1998–2000	2000–	2002–
Bore (mm)	99	87.5	101	101
Stroke (mm)	70.5	70.5	70.5	70.5
Capacity (cc)	1,085	848	1,130	1,130
Compression ratio	10.3:1	10.3:1	10.3:1	10.3:1
Horsepower DIN	80@6,750rpm	70@7,000rpm	85@6,750rpm	85@6,750rpm
Overall width	920mm (36.2in)	920mm (36.2in)	920mm (36.2in)	980mm (38.6in)
Overall length	2,196mm (86.5in)	2,196mm (86.5in)	2,196mm (86.5in)	2,180mm (85.9in)
Wheelbase	1,509mm (59.4in)	1,509mm (59.4in)	1,509mm (59.4in)	1,501mm (59.1in)
Weight including oil and fuel	243kg (536lb)	249kg (549lb)	249kg (549lb)	253kg (558lb)
Top speed	195kph (121mph)	185kph (115mph)	195kph (121mph)	192kph (119mph)

The new ellipsoidal headlights provided the R1150GS with a new face, and the Telelever was machined to replicate traditional forks. (BMW)

a while, primarily to use up the supply of earlier components, as happened so often in the history of BMW motorcycles.

The R1150GS

The R1150GS was released to coincide with the 20th anniversary of the *Gelände Strasse*, and to celebrate the production of nearly 115,000 examples of the GS genre. The GS was always promoted as a large adventure and long-distance enduro, the Range Rover of motorcycles, and the 1150 expanded on and improved this concept. The engine displacement was enlarged slightly, and developments were aimed at increasing power and torque, particularly torque in the mid-range. But it wasn't only the engine that was updated; the chassis and styling also received attention. The resulting R1150GS was a significant improvement over its predecessor, and undoubtedly the finest example yet of the *Gelände Strasse*.

The R1150GS utilised many components from newer models in the R259 Boxer family. The 101mm cylinders (but without polished fins) came from the recently released R1200C Cruiser, while the crankshaft, cylinder heads, and magnesium valve covers were from the R1100S Sportster. The camshaft had milder cam timing, to fatten the torque curve further, and

the engine management was the newer Motronic MA 2.4 system. There was also a larger oil cooler, this time from the R1100RT, and, to minimise weight, the 600-watt alternator and smaller 14Ah battery were from the R1100S.

About 50 per cent of the improvement in engine performance was attributable to the new exhaust system, with two 45mm (up from 38mm) exhaust header pipes connected to a double tube (instead of one as before) and a pre-silencer housing the catalytic converter and oxygen sensor. The large single muffler was moved higher up to maintain the enduro image.

Shared with the sporting R1100S was the six-speed gearbox, although the sixth gear was raised to become an overdrive (as on the later R1150RT and R1150RS). Also from the R1100S came the smaller diameter (165mm) hydraulic clutch. While BMW claimed the six-speed transmission provided improved shifting and precision, in reality this gearbox wasn't any improvement.

What was improved on the R1150GS over the R1100GS was the chassis. While retaining the engine and transmission housing as load-bearing components for the front and rear subframes, the front Telelever was the lighter R1100S type. This included machined fork sliders designed to emulate conventional upside

112

down forks, and an assembled, rather than cast, A-arm. Around 1kg (2.2lb) of unsprung weight was saved. The front and rear shock absorbers were unchanged, but the rear Paralever was redesigned with a shorter swingarm (as on the R1150RT and RS) to accommodate the longer transmission housing. Unique to the R1150GS were new aluminium footpeg plates to reinforce the swingarm pivot and prevent rear frame failure. Apart from a slightly different rear wheel hub, the cross-spoked wheels and Brembo triple disc braking system were as before, although the front brake pads for the four-piston calipers were now sintered metal rather than organic. ABS II was an option, and could be manually deactivated for off-road use.

Central to the style of the R1150GS was a makeover designed to set the new model apart from its predecessor. Neither the R1150GS or R1100GS were particularly beautiful machines, but the newer edition cleverly created a more purposeful image. While retaining the beak-like upper front wheel cover with oil cooler air intake, this was integrated with the 22.1-litre (4.8gal) fuel tank. The most significant visual update was the headlight set-up, with two asymmetrical ellipsoidal headlights, similar to those of the R1100S, providing a new 'face'. The larger light was an H7 low beam, with a smaller H1 high beam. The new instrument cluster was situated slightly further back, and there was an optional Rider Information Display. The windshield was adjustable, or could be removed altogether if true open air motorcycling was required. Unchanged was the separately mounted handlebar, although this was wider for increased leverage, and there were the newer generation handlebar switches and controls first introduced on the R1200C and R1100S. So well thought out was the design that there were no changes to the R1150GS for 2001 and 2002. For 2003, however, the R1150GS received the updated six-speed gearbox, while the optional ABS became the new Integral system.

Although not really a serious off-road machine, when fitted with some of the optional touring equipment (panniers and top box) the R1150GS presented a viable alternative to pure street and touring motorcycles. On the move, the disadvantage of weight and size was cleverly disguised, and in the manner of all GSs the

Apart from new colours there were no changes to the R1150GS for 2002. (BMW)

115

The Paris-Dakar R900RR

Although the Paris-Dakar minimum weight regulations from 1999 favoured single cylinder motorcycles, BMW decided to produce an RR boxer twin desert racer. Ostensibly based on the R1100GS, this ran alongside the successful F650RR singles. As with the earlier Paris-Dakar twins, the preparation of the R900RR was entrusted to tuning specialists HPN, and the RR debuted at the 1999 Tunisian Rally in the hands of Oscar Gallardo. Two machines were then prepared for the 2000 Paris-Dakar-Cairo rally. With the regulations stipulating 190kg (419lb) for up to 900cc, and 200kg (441lb) for anything larger, it was decided to run the machines as 900cc.

Because of the inconsistent fuel quality in Africa, the RR ran with twin Bing 40mm carburettors with quick release float bowls. The power was around 90bhp, and the ignition could be manually retarded if required. A simpler CDI set-up (with complete back-up system) replaced the digital ignition. Rather than utilise the existing BMW frame and Telelever, HPN installed the race-prepared engine in their steel multi-tube frame with alloy rear subframe. They then equipped the RR with White Power 48mm upside down forks, and a White Power PDS shock absorber with the single-sided Paralever swingarm. Wheel travel was 300mm (11.8in) front and rear, and the steering geometry was based on that of the successful boxer racers of the 1980s, with 28.3° of rake, 116mm (4.6in) of trail, and a 1,597mm (62.3in) wheelbase. An Öhlins steering damper fitted above the top fork yoke, and braking was by Brembo, with a single disc and four-piston caliper on each wheel.

In the 2000 Paris-Dakar-Cairo rally, the works R900RR was ridden by John Deacon and American Jimmy Lewis. A Plymouth motorcycle dealer, Deacon was a veteran Paris-Dakar competitor, but poor rear suspension and faulty foam rubber tyre mousses (used instead of inner tubes) handicapped the R900RR. Although the abundance of long straight sections favoured the twin, delays caused Deacon to crash on Day 5 while trying to make up time, while Lewis managed a gallant third, mostly on half throttle.

For the UAE Desert Challenge, or Dubai rally – a prelude to the 2001 Paris-Dakar – Deacon rode an 1,100cc version, but Lewis won on the 900. While the dry weight of the 900 was now down to 190kg (419lb), developments saw a new fuel tank layout in order to centralise the huge mass. The main tank held 34 litres (7.5gal), with 10 litres (2.2gal) in rear pannier tanks, and a further 10 litres under the seat. There was a new torque arm extending from the rear hub to the main frame, but the most significant improvement was a wind tunnel designed fairing that incorporated the front mudguard. This was 30–40 per cent more efficient, provided front wheel downforce, and contributed to improved high speed behaviour.

The team was expanded to include Juan 'Nani' Roma and Cyril Despres, but the course was slower and more technical than the previous year, favouring the lighter singles. An electrical fault delayed Deacon, Roma crashed out while holding third, and Lewis broke a collarbone on the run in to Dakar. Deacon managed sixth, while Lewis remounted and limped home to seventh. Capable of around 200kph (124mph), the fully wet 300kg (661lb) R900RR was a formidable desert weapon, but it wasn't destined to repeat the victory of its illustrious predecessors.

British rider John Deacon rode the factory R900RR in the 2000 and 2001 Paris-Dakar rallies, finishing sixth in 2001. (Mac McDiarmid)

R1150GS was a surprisingly good street motorcycle. There was no disguising that the R1150GS was large, but it was the king of dual-purpose bikes.

The R1150GS Adventure

As affluence and the demand for exciting leisure activities increased, niche marketing became the byword for increasing sales in a more competitive environment. BMW was intent on expanding motorcycle sales and production, and the establishment of a wider variety of niche models led to the next stage in the evolution of the R1150GS, the R1150GS Adventure.

Released at the Milan Show in September 2001, the Adventure was the ultimate motorcycle for those dreaming of riding to the remotest parts of the world. The engine was unchanged from the excellent unit of the R1150GS, but to prove the Adventure was a true exploring machine and not just a pretty face it could be modified to run only low octane fuel if required. For those who dared to venture into the depths of Africa, Asia, America, or

Australia, an optional engine management coding plug could be inserted into the ignition map. This enabled the engine to run on RON 91 regular fuel without risking damage. The alternator was also the larger 700-watt type, with a 19Ah battery. Compared to the R1150GS, the six-speed gearbox included a shorter sixth gear, with an optional lower first gear available if slow speed use in difficult terrain was envisaged. For 2003 the gearbox was updated to the newer type.

Developments to the suspension were aimed at providing improved off-road performance. Spring travel for the Showa shock absorbers was increased by 20mm, to 210mm (8.3in) on the front and 220mm (8.7in) at the rear, and an innovation for a BMW motorcycle was the White Power WAD rear shock absorber that provided increased damping in concert with greater spring deflection. Spring adjustment was by a hydraulic hand wheel, with screw adjusted rebound damping. The braking was also upgraded, with new EVO brake calipers on the front, although, unlike other EVO disc models,

The R1150GS Adventure, fully equipped with optional aluminium luggage. (Ian Falloon)

117

the brake disc diameter remained at the smaller 305mm. The brake hoses were upgraded with flexible steel housings, and there was the option of ABS II, which could be disengaged for off-road use. From 2003 the ABS was the updated Integral set-up.

In many respects the R1150GS Adventure replicated the function of the earlier R80 G/S Paris-Dakar. Although it could accommodate two if required, the seat was set up for the rider, who could sit closer to the tank on rough terrain or further back on touring sections. The windshield was also larger, 120mm (4.7in) wider at the bottom and 130mm (5.1in) longer, and the front mudguard was likewise wider and longer. Handlebar and hand protectors were standard, and the aluminium engine sump protection plate was larger and positioned further back. There was also a 12-volt socket in the cockpit to power important accessories such as GPS.

Like the earlier Paris-Dakar replica and R80 G/S, striking visual features distinguished the Adventure from the R1150GS. The engine valve covers were anodised blue, and the wheel rims epoxy-plated blue, while the colours of white aluminium with a red and grey seat, or black with a black and mandarin seat, were distinctive. And the extensive range of special

accessories allowed the Adventure to be tailored to suit the most demanding circumstances. These extended to a 30-litre (6.6gal) fuel tank, and voluminous and robust aluminium luggage system specifically developed for the Adventure. The side cases accepted 75 litres (39 litres on the right and 36 litres on the left), with the top case providing 30 litres. The case racks could also be folded out to provide a load surface when the cases weren't fitted. Other accessories included cylinder protection bars and protective grilles for the lights. The R1150GS Adventurer could therefore be outfitted as the ultimate exploring motorcycle, even if it never ventured far off the beaten track.

If there was any criticism that could be levelled at the R1150GS range, it was excessive weight and bulk. With this in mind, BMW's designers set about redesigning the GS and a new R1200GS was released early in 2004. The new boxer engine had lighter crankcases, a balance shaft driven by spur gears from the crankshaft, and produced 100 bhp. Ligher wheels, Telelever, Paralever, and differential, saw the overall weight reduced to 225 kg (496 lb). This new generation GS would undoubtedly herald another chapter in the boxer twin story.

Opposite: As a motorcycle to explore beyond traditional limits, the R1150GS Adventure had no peer. (BMW)

The R1200GS was the first new boxer since the R259 of 1993, and shared virtually nothing with its predecessor. (BMW)

10 Roadster

A significant phenomenon of the 1990s was the rise of the naked motorcycle. In a world of increasing plastic coverage, the naked motorcycle represented a return to simpler concepts; and while BMW was a pioneer of the factory-fitted sport and touring fairing, it always had a strong tradition of producing standard motorcycles. Although overshadowed by the Sporting and Touring variants, the best-selling BMW motorcycles over the years were often the basic and unadorned models. For example, the naked R100R was the most popular BMW motorcycle in 1992. The R100R was largely a parts bin special, and when it came to producing the R1100R BMW pursued a similar policy. The resulting R1100R, released for the 1995 model year, was hardly a beautiful creation, but it was effective, and proved even more successful than the R1100GS.

The R1100R and R850R

Rather than utilising the high performance engine of the R1100RS, BMW's engineers reasoned that the lower power, higher torque R1100GS engine was more suitable for the roadster. Even the exhaust system was shared, and the only difference between the engines of the R1100R and R1100GS was the location of the oil cooler. Instead of a single oil cooler under the headlight, the R had two smaller oil coolers mounted on either side above the cylinder heads. Alongside the R1100R was an entry-level R850R, with a downsized A62 engine. While retaining the same stroke, this 850cc A62 engine had smaller pistons and valves (32 and 27mm). There was also a lower performing 34bhp version available in selected markets, but the R850R didn't meet with the same enthusiastic response in the showroom as

its larger brother. Although the power output of the A62 engine was respectable, the reduction in torque, from 71lb/ft at 5,250rpm to 57lb/ft at 5,500rpm, seriously impeded on-the-road performance.

Also from the R1100GS came the essential frame components. These included the separately mounted two-piece aluminium handlebar, but with the Telelever A-arm and front and rear shock absorbers of the R1100RS. The wheel travel was also identical to the RS, but the combination of various suspension components resulted in new steering geometry. There was a 27° steering head angle, with 127mm (5.0in) of trail, and a hydraulic steering damper quelled instability caused by the lighter loading on the front wheel. The cast wheels were from the R1100RS, although cross-spoked wire wheels with alloy rims were available as an option. These were similar to those of the R1100GS, except that the front was an 18in and not a 19in. Also from the R1100RS were the Brembo front brakes, although the rear disc was the smaller 276mm unit of the GS.

BMW's designers also set out to provide the R1100R with a different face to the RS and GS. From its small round headlight to the 21-litre (4.6gal) steel fuel tank and deeply scalloped seat, the R1100R emphasised round shapes. The seat was adjustable for height, from 760–800mm (29.9–31.5in), but the puritanically basic cockpit (without a tachometer and clock) and cheap plastic instrument housing did little to impart any image of quality. Options extended to anti-lock brakes, additional instruments, windshield, and a black Telelever and engine kit. Uncovered by a fairing, the entire Telelever front suspension was on display and contributed to an

Continuing on from the R100R was the R1100R released for 1995, which coincided with a resurgence of interest in naked motorcycles. (BMW)

120

Unlike earlier standard boxers, the R1100R could be ergonomically tailored for the rider, with a variety of seat heights available. The cockpit was very basic. (Australian Motorcycle News)

unconventional appearance. All in all the R1100R was a strange looking beast, but it was undeniably competent, and possibly the best-handling boxer of them all. Even the most sceptical were convinced, and the R1100R was an outstanding success, eclipsing all other variants of the new boxer. Between 1996 and 2000, 53,685 examples of the R1100R and R850R were sold.

In an effort to overcome some of the criticisms of the aesthetics, during 1997 an aluminium instrument support replaced the ugly plastic unit, the chrome-plated instrument console was altered to include a tachometer and clock, and the headlight was enlarged and provided with a chrome-plated shell. These updates were a welcome improvement.

For 1998 there was a 75th Anniversary edition, and a further facelift included chrome-plated mirrors and handlebar weights, with the levers, oil cooler covers, and rear subframe silver powder-coated. After the release of the improved R1150R for 2001, R1100R and R850R classic 'Special Model' editions were offered. These were an ivory retro-style model, featuring wire-spoked wheels and chrome-plated valve covers. The R1100R Special Model ended during 2001, but the R850R version continued for 2002, still based on the older model.

The Telelever front suspension was unique to the R1100R, including the separately mounted handlebar of the R1100GS, with the R1100RS A-arm. Above each cylinder was an oil cooler. (Australian Motorcycle News)

Options were always available for the R1100R, including the wire-spoked wheels and screen of this example. (Australian Motorcycle News)

R1100R, R850R, and R1150R
specifications

	R1100R	**R850R**	**R1150R**	**R850R**
Years	1995–9	1995–2002	2001–	2003–
Bore (mm)	99	87.5	101	87.5
Stroke (mm)	70.5	70.5	70.5	70.5
Capacity (cc)	1085	848	1130	848
Compression ratio	10.3:1	10.3:1	10.3:1	10.3:1
Horsepower DIN	80@6,750rpm	70@7,000rpm	85@6,750rpm	70@7,000rpm
Overall width	898mm (35.4in)	898mm (35.4in)	970mm (38.2in)	940mm (37in)
Overall length	2,197mm (86.6in)	2,197mm (86.6in)	2,170mm (85.5in)	2,170mm (85.5in)
Wheelbase	1,487mm (58.6in)	1,487mm (58.6in)	1,487mm (58.6in)	1,487mm (58.6in)
Weight including oil and fuel	235kg (518lb)	235kg (518lb)	238kg (525lb)	238kg (525lb)
Top speed	197kph (122mph)	187kph (116mph)	197kph (122mph)	187kph (116mph)

The R1150R and R850R

Further revisions to the roadster resulted in the improved R1150R for 2001. Stylist David Robb provided a significant makeover, altering the roadster functionally and aesthetically to create one of the finest renditions by any manufacturer of the naked bike concept. Continuing the theme of the R1100R, the higher torque engine of the R1150R came from the R1150GS, with the cylinder heads and crankshaft from the sporting

The styling of the R1150R was more integrated than its predecessor, and the Telelever A-arm was incorporated as part of the style. Upgraded wheels and brakes meant that the handling was even more surefooted. (BMW)

R1100S, Motronic MA 2.4 digital engine management, and magnesium valve covers. As with the R1150GS, most of the engine performance increase was attributed to the stainless steel exhaust system. The oil cooling system was revamped, with the twin oil coolers now contained in aerodynamic ducts in the sides of the fuel tank. These now looked integrated rather than an afterthought. The six-speed gearbox and hydraulically operated clutch also came from the R1150GS, except for the lower sixth gear of the R1100S. As with other boxers, from 2003 the R1150R received the modified six-speed gearbox.

Also from the R1150GS came the rear frame set-up, with aluminium footpeg support plates (with R1100S footpegs) providing additional rigidity. New was an R1100RS-style tubular steel A-arm for the Telelever front suspension, designed to complement the front end aesthetics, and a new single-sleeve front shock absorber. An adjustment bolt provided infinite rebound adjustment, and the compression damping was now linear (as opposed to progressive on the R1100R). The rear suspension with shorter Paralever swingarm was carried over from the R1150GS, and the wheels were the 17in lighter double-spoke type of the

R1100S. Also new was the EVO front brake with updated Brembo-Tokico four-piston calipers. The front brake discs were now 320mm, and the new generation Integral ABS was an option. This was the partial system, also featured on the R1150RS from 2002, and for 2003 the brake lines were braided steel.

Apart from the headlight and instrument panel, everything about the bodywork was new for the R1150R, including the two-piece front mudguard and larger, 20.4-litre (4.5gal) fuel tank. As with other boxers the seat could also be tailored to suit a wide variety of riders, with seat heights from 770mm (30.3in) to 830mm (32.7in) available. The handlebar was wider, lower, and further forward to provide a more sporting riding position, and this additional weight on the front wheel saw the loss of the R1100R's steering damper. The styling of the R1150R incorporated a uniformity of line that was absent on the earlier R1100R. The result, purposeful and elegant, was one of the most successful renditions of the new boxer. For the 2003 model year, the R850R made a return. Still in 70 or 34bhp guises, this now featured a six-speed transmission and looked visually similar to the 1,150cc version.

The R1150R Rockster

Displayed at the Munich Intermot in September 2002 was a concept roadster boxer. Another example of David Robb's attempt to expand the customer base through niche marketing, this was envisaged as a more aggressive rendition of the naked boxer. With its matt-black highlighting and distinctive two-tone paint, the roadster was designed to appeal to a younger demographic than the usual boxer buyer. As with other boxers, it combined components from a number of models. The essential basis was the R1150R, but with some of the sporting R1100S components, and the twin ellipsoidal headlights from the R1150GS. The machined, black Telelever fork tubes, and wider 5.50 x 17in rear wheel came from the R1100S, as did instruments.

A specific sporting front mudguard was fitted, and the response was so positive that in October 2003 it was announced that the concept roadster would go into production during 2003. The production version was called the R1150R Rockster, and was the first model to feature the new dual spark plug ignition cylinder heads that would feature on all 2004 model year boxers. The dual ignition was claimed to reduce emissions and improve fuel consumption by five per cent. During 2003 a special R1150R Rockster Edition 80 was also available, created to celebrate the boxer's 80th anniversary. Only 2003 were produced, in white and metallic black, and came complete with commemorative badge and certificate.

The positive response to the concept roadster led to its release as the Rockster during 2003. Evo brakes with larger diameter discs, R1100S-style Telelever, and R1150GS headlights set the Rockster apart from the R1150R. (Ian Falloon)

11 Extremes: cruisers and sportsters

While the R1100GS, R1100R, and R1100RT were essentially variations on the RS theme, for 1998 the R259 boxer took a turn in a radical new direction. This was the cruiser. The following year saw a reversal in direction with the reintroduction of the sporting boxer. While the cruiser was a new concept, the sportster continued a tradition initiated in 1960 with the R50S and R69S but which had since lapsed with the demise of the R100CS in 1984. These two models at the extreme ends of the motorcycling spectrum expanded the boxer twin line-up. Already the R259 was the most successful BMW motorcycle of all time, and the increase in model range to cater for more specialised use only boosted the boxer's appeal.

The cruiser

The motorcycle market changed dramatically during the late 1980s and early 1990s, and the primary casualties were sportsbikes. This didn't affect BMW unduly as it wasn't specifically involved in the sportsbike business, but the growth segment of cruisers, particularly in the US and Germany, caused some concern. Cruiser sales were almost doubling annually in America, and the expansion was even more apparent in Germany. Because of this changing marketplace, early in 1994 BMW's directors sanctioned the development of a cruiser.

The traditional American cruiser was the Harley-Davidson large capacity V-twin, which the Japanese manufacturers assiduously copied. But it was neither feasible, nor part of the BMW psychology, to pursue this approach. The company already had a suitable powerplant in

the R259 boxer, and this could be easily adapted for the particular requirements of a cruiser. There was no need for the engine to rev hard, but it needed an extremely fat torque curve, so some fundamental changes were made. The first step was to increase the engine capacity to 1,170cc, through a larger bore (101mm) and longer stroke (73mm). The valve sizes were reduced to 34mm inlet and 29mm exhaust, with lower lift (8.23mm) and shorter duration (256°) camshafts; and the intake manifold diameter was reduced to 35mm, as was the throttle butterfly diameter. The engine management system was the Motronic MA 2.4, and incorporated an automatic choke.

On a cruiser, the exhaust system is integral to the classic style, and that on the R1200C combined a pre-muffler with catalytic converter, and twin silencers, at the same time adhering to the European standard of 80dB(A). BMW engineers nevertheless managed to impart the characteristic BMW throaty growl. With these developments, the cruiser engine produced only moderate power, but peak torque of 72lb/ft at only 3,000rpm. From 2,500 to 4,500rpm 66lb/ft was available, and the useful rev range was 1,500–6,500rpm, or 50kph (31mph) to 160kph (100mph) in top gear.

A hydraulically operated 165mm single-plate dry clutch led straight into the new five-speed gearbox. This was derived from the six-speed transmission of the four-cylinder K1200RS. As the swingarm was mounted on the tubular steel subframe and not the transmission housing it was more compact. The gearbox ratios were also specific to the cruiser, with a close first and second and a high fifth gear. The cruiser also

BMW ventured into new territory with the R1200C cruiser, creating another successful niche market. (BMW)

126

BMW Grafik Design VT-T

saw a return of the Monolever, with the drive shaft and two universal joints running inside the hollow swingarm. This was 90mm (3.5in) longer than the Paralever, and the single shock absorber was mounted centrally. Apart from allowing twin silencers, the most obvious by-product of the long swingarm was the long wheelbase. Although not considered ideal in more sporting machines, its length provided the cruiser with exceptional stability, and provided a lot of room on the motorcycle. The saddle-shaped seat was moved further back, with the footrests more forward.

The demands of the cruiser also called for a distinctive chassis design. While committed to the Telelever, the front aluminium subframe couldn't be easily disguised, so it was designed to be integral with the styling and image. Consequently the front subframe was finished in a pearl-gloss chrome, incorporating the two air intakes for the oil coolers. The engine and transmission were still load bearing, and the rear subframe was an inconspicuous steel tube structure. As the longer triangular control arm

was an important design feature, it was welded aluminium (instead of steel), and polished. The Telelever fork tubes, set at a cruiser-like rake of 29.5°, were also polished. Trail was a short 86mm (3.4in), and the single-sleeve gas-pressure shock absorber provided 144mm (5.7in) of spring travel. Rear shock absorber travel was 100mm (3.9in), and from November 1998 a softer spring was fitted. Later, for the 2000 model year, the original harder spring was available as an option.

As the wheels were crucial to the character of the motorcycle a lot of effort went into selecting an appropriate type. Balancing traditional looks with modern technology, they were a classic wire spoke with chrome-plated rims, and the usual BMW cross-spoke design. Wheel sizes too were cruiser inspired; a 2.50 x 18in on the front and 4.00 x 15in on the rear. In contrast to some other cruisers, though, the braking system of the R1200C was more than up to the task of hauling it down. Shared with the R1100GS, this included dual stainless steel 305mm discs with four-piston calipers, and a single 285mm disc

The R1200C chassis incorporated a Monolever rather than Paralever, with the swingarm bolting to the rear subframe instead of the transmission housing. (BMW)

Opposite: Intended primarily for the US market, the cruiser was all about projecting the right image. (BMW)

The attention to detail was staggering on the R1200C, extending from the retro-styled tail-light to the leather seat. (BMW)

(from the R1100RS) with dual piston caliper. ABS II was an option.

When establishing a design philosophy for the R1200C, David Robb successfully created a cruiser with a specific identity. While emphasising traditional, and nostalgic values, it was also innovative, stylish, functional, and fitted out with the highest quality components. Particular attention was paid to the side silhouette, with spaces left intentionally around the Telelever spring and Monolever to impart a feeling of transparency. As the engine was also a focal component the cylinder head covers were chrome-plated.

Attention to detail extended to the cruiser handlebar with new integrated controls and switches, while the only instrument above the round headlight was a speedometer, with 1950s-style numerals. The seat was intentionally conceived as a monoposto, for the rider alone, shaped like a saddle and finished in leather. From the 1999 model year there was an optional seat, with additional 20mm padding. As long distances weren't envisaged for this type of motorcycle the fuel tank was only 17 litres (3.7gal), and was adorned with a chrome-plated filler cap and surrounded by the matt-chrome plated frame and air intakes. In contrast to the lighter-weight materials featured on other models, the cruiser fuel tank, mudguards, and

sidecovers were steel, and provided an excellent basis for the carefully applied paint. As in earlier days, the female workers at Spandau carefully applied colour co-ordinated pinstripes to the tank and mudguards, accentuating the cruiser's classic image. In addition a wide range of options ensured that it could be outfitted and personalised in a manner similar to that of Harley-Davidson. There were lower and wider handlebars, windshield, and leather saddlebags.

Soon after its release the R1200C made a spectacular appearance with James Bond in the 007 thriller *Tomorrow Never Dies*, and during 1998 it was the best-selling BMW motorcycle. A similar R850C was offered during 1999, identical to the R1200C apart from the smaller displacement A62 engine. This proved less popular and was discontinued for 2002. Other variants were more successful. The Avantgarde version supplemented the Classic cruiser for 2000, featuring a black enamel finish for the engine and drivetrain, and graphitane (graphite and magnesium) for many of the previously chromed components ranging from the fork tubes to the A-arm and front and rear frames. This was to create a darker and more modern looking alternative to classic silver. The Avantgarde also featured a touring handlebar, combining features of the high cruiser handlebar and optional low sports handlebar.

Another variant of the R1200C was the Avantgarde, with lower handlebars and a black and graphitane accentuation. (BMW)

With its solo seat and small speedster fairing, the R1200C Independent further expanded the cruiser's appeal. (BMW)

The
R1200CL

The Cruiser line-up expanded beyond traditional boundaries with the release of the R1200CL luxury cruiser at the end of 2002. The idea of the CL was to incorporate touring features into the cruiser, creating a unique machine that combined the distinctive characteristics of both parent types. The engine, rear wheel drive, and fuel tank came from the R1200C, but most

Based on the R1200C cruiser, the R1200CL luxury tourer had a distinctive handlebar-mounted fairing with four headlights. (BMW)

other components were new, in particular the fairing, more powerful 840-watt alternator, and six-speed gearbox. This was the new generation Getrag-built unit, with softer mesh to reduce noise. Top gear was an overdrive, and instead of the usual gearshift lever the R1200CL had a rocking foot shifter.

The most distinctive feature of the CL was the new face, with the handlebar-mounted touring fairing extending back along separate fairings at the side to the tank, to create a fully integrated look. There were four headlights, two H1 for low and two H4 for high beam, and the aerodynamic design of the windshield included an upper edge cut-out, contoured like a wave to deflect air around the rider. The front mudguard extended down at the side, around the large front tyre, while the flatter

Telelever emphasised the cruiser look. Standard touring features included integral hard cases and a removable top box. As with other cruisers, the attention to detail in the choice of materials was outstanding. The pressure cast aluminium luggage rack was finished in white, as was the upper instrument panel, while the inside of the fairing was finished in the same material as the seat.

To provide exceptional touring ability, the chassis was unique to the CL and included extreme steering geometry. A Telelever, reconfigured from the ground up, provide a rake of 33.5°, with a huge 184mm (7.2in) of trail. The fork tubes were also further apart to accommodate the 150/80 x 16in front tyre. While front wheel travel was the same as the cruiser, the rear Monolever included a shock absorber with 120mm (4.7in) of

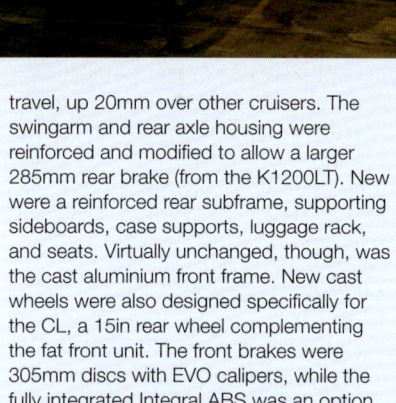

travel, up 20mm over other cruisers. The swingarm and rear axle housing were reinforced and modified to allow a larger 285mm rear brake (from the K1200LT). New were a reinforced rear subframe, supporting sideboards, case supports, luggage rack, and seats. Virtually unchanged, though, was the cast aluminium front frame. New cast wheels were also designed specifically for the CL, a 15in rear wheel complementing the fat front unit. The front brakes were 305mm discs with EVO calipers, while the fully integrated Integral ABS was an option.

Other new features were the low-maintenance, sealed 19Ah battery, a second power socket, and electronic

speedometer and tachometer with redesigned faces. The rider and passenger seats were separate, with cruiser-style footboards for the rider. Optional equipment extended to cruise control, heated handlebars and seat, CD player, cup holders, and on-board communication. Undeniably aimed at the American market, in many respects the R1200CL was similar in function to the four-cylinder K1200LT. Both emphasised luxury and comfort, but with the R1200CL style was also paramount. And despite its size, weight, and moderate power, the R1200CL was surprisingly capable as a supremely comfortable long distance hauler.

Standard features on the R1200CL included integral cases and top box. (Ian Falloon)

133

R1200C, R850C, and R1200CL *specifications*

	R1200C	R850C	R1200CL
Years	1998–	1999–2001	2003–
Bore (mm)	101	87.5	101
Stroke (mm)	73	70.5	73
Capacity (cc)	1,170	848	1,170
Compression ratio	10:1	10.3:1	10:1
Horsepower DIN	61@5,000rpm	50@5,250rpm	61@5,000rpm
Overall width	1,050mm (41.4in)	1,050mm (41.4in)	853mm (33.6in)
Overall length	2,340mm (92.2in)	2,340mm (92.2in)	2,415mm (95.1in)
Wheelbase	1,650mm (65.0in)	1,650mm (65.0in)	1,641mm (64.6in)
Weight including oil and fuel	256kg (564lb)	256kg (564lb)	308kg (679lb)
Top speed	168kph (104mph)	155kph (96mph)	165kph (102mph)

A third version, the Independent, became available for 2001. This had a solo seat, oval mirrors, new wheels, additional small fog lamps, and a small speedster-type handlebar fairing. The alternator cover, new oil cooler intakes, levers, and fluid reservoirs were chrome-plated. The aluminium wheels were two-piece, with three-spoke inner hubs connected by titanium bolts replacing the usual cross-spoke wheels. For 2003 the cast aluminium wheels were an option for the R1200C, and the Independent was available with a small passenger seat. Also during 2003 another cruiser variant was released, the strangely named Montauk. Intended to fill a gap between the R1200C Classic and R1200CL luxury cruiser, the Montauk debuted several updates that would feature on 2004 models, including the twin spark plug cylinder heads, new five-speed gearbox, and uprated EVO brake system. The 16in front, and 15in rear wheels were from the R1200CL, and the equipment included a small screen, dual-stacked headlights, new sidecovers, and small passenger seat on top of the rear mudguard.

The R1100S

As the 'S' designation was significant within the historical context of the boxer, it was no surprise to see the R259 develop into the R1100S. During 1994 David Robb proposed a concept R1100S boxer, which was displayed at the Cologne Show that year. This had cross-spoked wire wheels, but the integrated fairing and fuel tank set the scene for the eventual production version of 1998. In the style of the earlier classic R69S and R90S, the R1100S was still a sport-touring motorcycle, with the emphasis on sport rather than touring. With more power and less weight than the R1100RS, the R1100S was the most sporting and best-handling boxer yet.

Although the 1,100cc engine was basically that of the R1100RS, modifications were made to improve the power output without sacrificing the torque curve. New pistons provided an increase in the compression ratio, and a plate-type air filter, instead of circular, ensured improved breathing. As the safe engine speed rose to 8,400rpm, there were stronger, forged con-rods, while the oil circulation in the crankcases was improved. The oil capacity went up by 0.35 litres to 4.1 litres. Visibly distinguishing the R1100S engine were new cylinder head bolts with three protruding fins on the lower side, and 'Magnesium' designations. These cylinder head covers saved 800g.

From the R1200C came the newer Bosch Motronic MA 2.4 digital engine management system, but around 70 per cent of the extra power was attributed to the new stainless steel exhaust. The exhaust manifold diameter was up to 45mm (from the R1100RS's 38mm), and connected with an interference pipe before merging into the large pre-muffler housing and the fully controlled three-way catalytic converter. An increased muffler volume reduced counter-pressure while still maintaining the characteristic throaty boxer sound. The twin mufflers positioned directly beneath the tail looked more sporting, even if they were undeniably derivative of the Ducati 916 set-up. The resulting engine was the most powerful production boxer ever built by BMW.

From the new K1200RS came the hydraulically operated single-plate dry clutch and six-speed gearbox. As the Paralever swingarm rested on the new central frame rather than the gearbox, the gearbox housing was more compact than before. To minimise weight the standard battery was a smaller 14Ah type (saving 1.4kg), and there was a smaller

Re-establishing the boxer Sport theme, the R1100S took the new boxer in a completely different direction from the cruiser. (BMW)

The R1100S was the most sporting and best-handling boxer to date. (Australian Motorcycle News)

600-watt alternator (saving 0.97kg). If additional electrical equipment was specified, like Integral ABS or heated handgrips, the larger 19Ah battery and 700-watt alternator were required.

Although the engine for the R1100S was slightly upgraded over that of other boxers, the chassis was completely revamped to provide better handling and stability. The Telelever was retained, but with machined fork sliders about 1kg of unsprung weight was saved. The front shock absorber was a single-sleeve gas-pressure unit providing 110mm (4.3in) of spring travel. Rebound damping was infinitely adjustable by a knob while the rider was on the move. The more sporting geometry was specific to the R1100S, with a steering head angle of 25° and trail of 100mm (3.9in). It was also claimed that with an 85kg (187lb) rider on board the R1100S could lean over 50° before grounding the engine.

The four-piece frame was quite different to that on other boxers. The engine and gearbox were still load bearing, but an additional welded aluminium central frame and a die-cast aluminium front frame provided increased rigidity between the steering head and swingarm. The rear subframe remained in tubular steel, as it only had to support the seat and luggage rack. The central gas-pressure shock absorber connected the bottom of the Paralever swingarm to the top of the central aluminium frame and provided 130mm (5.1in) of spring travel. Spring preload was hydraulically adjustable, with 40 positions, and rebound damping was adjustable with a screw.

The R1100S was the first boxer to feature the new-style 17in five double-spoke aluminium cast wheels, and while the rear wheel was a wider 5.00in an even wider 5.50in was an option. This allowed for a 180/55 ZR 17 tyre. Apart from the smaller (16mm) master cylinder, the front braking system was the same as other boxers, with the smaller 276mm rear disc of the R1100GS. From 2001 the front brakes were upgraded with EVO calipers and 320mm discs. ABS was also an option, with the partially integrated Integral system from 2001.

With its wind tunnel developed four-piece sporting fairing, the R1100S maintained an individual sporting look initiated by the earlier R90S. The fairing, with integrated direction indicators and hand protectors, also offered

R1100S specifications

	R1100S
Years	1999–
Bore (mm)	99
Stroke (mm)	70.5
Capacity (cc)	1,085
Compression ratio	11.3:1
Horsepower DIN	98@7,500rpm
Overall width	880mm (34.7in)
Overall length	2,180mm (85.9in)
Wheelbase	1,478mm (58.2in)
Weight including oil and fuel	229kg (505lb)
Top speed	226kph (140mph)

The R1100S Telelever front end was designed to emulate more conventional upside down forks. The wheels were a new design. (Cycle World)

excellent rider protection, and above the typically BMW kidney-shaped oil cooler intakes was a new headlight set-up. This incorporated asymmetric dual headlights, a larger ellipsoidal H 7 for low beam and an automotive-type smaller H 1 high beam. Accentuating the sporting nature was a narrow, low handlebar, consisting of two separate forged aluminium units connecting to the vertical tube beneath the fork bridge. The cockpit was finished in black, with new instruments, while a large plastic shell disguised an 18-litre (4gal) aluminium fuel tank. Further weight saving measures extended to a carbon-fibre front mudguard. With footpegs moved further back than on the R1100RS, the riding position was more sport-touring, not unlike that of the older air-cooled R100RS, but with the rider enveloped by the bodywork. Options extended to a higher handlebar and screen, a black-painted engine and transmission, and a sport package, which included a steering damper and longer shock absorbers, raising the R1100S 18mm at the front and 20mm at the rear. The sport package increased the safe lean angle to 52°, and included a longer side stand.

Although it endeavoured to emulate the character of the magnificent earlier S-series, by 1999 motorcycles were more specialised, and the categories more polarised. Sporting motorcycles were harder edged, much lighter, and more powerful than their predecessors. In the 1960s and 1970s the gap between pure sporting and touring motorcycles hadn't been so large, but by the time the R1100S was released a huge chasm separated them. Touring bikes were larger and more luxurious, a dichotomy BMW was comfortable filling, but sporting motorcycles were now more racing oriented. The R1100S found itself in the middle ground, unable to compete with the current crop of race replicas, and without a true sporting identity. Undeniably capable, the R1100S was undoubtedly the finest-handling boxer twin yet, but it didn't manage to capture the market in the same way that the GS, R, RT, or even the cruiser had. At a time when BMW motorcycle sales were increasing dramatically, R1100S production of 20,000 between 1998 and 2002 was little more than that of the classic R90S 25 years earlier. To become a true successor to the R90S, the boxer needed to be more powerful, and considerably lighter.

The Boxer Cup *and* Boxer Cup *Replica*

Soon after the release of the R1100S, the French and Belgian BMW distributors set up a series of celebrity races with R1100Ss. These were initially support events for the FIM World Championship, and considerable prize money attracted several well-known racing stars, notably Randy Mamola, Kevin Schwantz, and Luca Cadalora. It grew into a competitive series for 2001 when former World Superbike star Stéphane Mertens won, and expanded to eight races and was called the International Boxer Cup for 2002. Mertens was again victorious. For 2003 there were nine rounds, the first at the Daytona 200. Robert Panichi won at Daytona, Mugello, and Sachsenring, with other victories shared by Thomas Hinterreiter, Andy Hoffman, and Sébastien Legrelle.

The Boxer Cup was notable in that the machines were all very similar, with only minimal modifications to the exhaust and engine management system permitted. To provide increased ground clearance and a wider rear tyre, the sport package was

A limited number of Boxer Cup Replicas were produced for 2003, with sporting suspension and different graphics. (BMW)

fitted, but the performance was remarkably similar to the stock R1100S. A production Boxer Cup Replica was also available for the 2003 model year. This was a standard R1100S, but with the sport package, carbon-fibre reinforced cylinder head covers, engine spoiler, and rear seat cover. Specific decals, including a Randy Mamola signature, set the Boxer Cup Replica apart, and for some markets there was also a Boxer Cup model, without the special decals, spoiler, seat cowl, or carbon-fibre valve covers.

139

Released in January 2004, the R1200 GS featured a new engine and gearbox, and an updated Telelever and Paralever. (BMW)

BMW BOXER TWINS EPILOGUE

As BMW celebrated the eightieth anniversary of Max Friz's first boxer twin, it was obvious that a new generation twin was waiting in the wings. The post Second World War era had seen three distinct engine developments, each with a long production life. Not surprisingly, these designs were also representative of the era in which they were conceived and produced. The Type 252, 267 and 268 engine, that lasted from 1951 through until 1969, was an expensive unit that maintained BMW's luxury image through some very difficult years. If it wasn't for this engine it is doubtful BMW would have survived as a company during the 1960s as it also powered the 700 car that initiated the success the company enjoys today.

As motorcycle sales stagnated towards the end of the 1960s, and the Earles fork twins appeared dated, BMW responded with the /5. Again, this was the right machine at the right time, and with the higher performance R90S and some racing success, BMW began to shed its image as a producer of staid and boring motorcycles. Only the strength of the German currency towards the end of the 1970s and early 1980s dented the success of this new generation air-cooled boxer. Its model life of 27 years eclipsed its illustrious predecessor, and while the four-cylinder K-series was intended to replace the twin, the twin bounced back with a vengeance in 1993.

The third generation post-war boxer, the R259, has not only continued where the air-cooled A10 engine finished, it has been developed into a variety of models. In response to a marketplace demanding more variety, the R259 has become cruiser, off-road motorcycle, roadster, sportster and tourer. Production has increased to previously unprecedented levels, but with the design a decade old it is beginning to show its age. In the past BMW would have continued producing obsolete designs to suit their established clientele, but today the emphasis is on continual expansion. In January 2004, the much anticipated new boxer was unveiled in the R1200GS. Lighter, and more powerful than its predecessor, the R1200GS also incorporated updated electrics (the Single Wire System) and a balance shaft to smooth any vibration. This is the boxer that will carry on the tradition, and see BMW through the next decade.

140

Index